1000
Cross Stitch Motifs

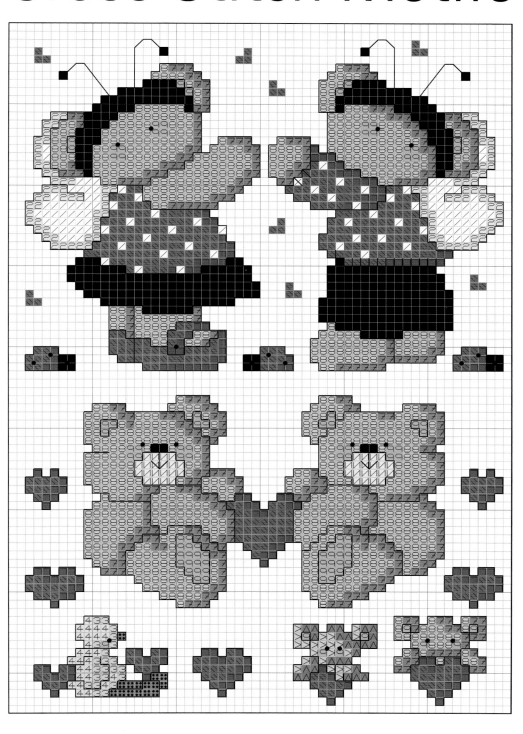

A huge thank you to my mum who has always inspired and encouraged me in all my creative projects, right from when I was very young.

1000
Cross Stitch Motifs

SHARON WELCH

SEARCH PRESS

This edition first published 2018

Search Press Limited
Wellwood, North Farm Road,
Tunbridge Wells, Kent TN2 3DR

Originally published in Great Britain 2013

Text and motif designs copyright © Sharon Welch
2013

Photographs by Search Press Studios

Photographs and book design copyright
© Search Press Ltd 2013

Print ISBN: 978-1-78221-586-8

Suppliers

If you have difficulty in obtaining any of the
materials and equipment mentioned in this
book, then please visit the Search Press website
for details of suppliers: www.searchpress.com

Printed in China through Asia Pacific Offset

Acknowledgements

First of all, I would like to give special thanks
to DMC for supplying the threads, fabrics and
other sewing materials, and my thanks go to
DMC's Cara Ackerman too for keeping me up to
date with samples of the latest range of threads,
fabrics, beads, and other sewing stuff. Thanks
also to all the editorial staff at Search Press for
making this book possible.

Page 1

The chart from page 176

Page 3

The chart from page 91

Opposite

*These mini motifs are worked from the
following charts:*

Flower pot and duck: page 54.

*Basket with rabbit: page 242, mixed and
matched with the small flowers from page
83 and the tulip from page 73.*

Watering can: page 159.

Cat: page 105

Contents

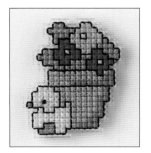

Introduction

Welcome to my cross-stitch world in which you will meet a fantastic range of cute, irresistible little friends. There are 1000 fun, adorable motifs for every occasion, including hearts, flowers, birds and animals, cup cakes and cookies, and all of them have been especially designed as individual mini motifs that can be used in samplers, on cards and for gifts, home items, garments and a range of accessories.

The first section of this book offers advice on what materials are required, with helpful stitch diagrams and practical information on techniques and how to start. The motifs follow on and have been arranged around themes so that you can find just what you want for any project. The only stitches you will need to know in order to work the carefully charted designs are cross stitch, back stitch and French knots – three perfect stitches for those with little, or no embroidery experience – and there is much here for more seasoned stitchers, with an inspiring range of beautiful designs to mix and match.

Exploring this book will be just the start of your cross-stitch adventure. You will soon discover the joys of creating something that is truly your own by mixing and matching the designs. I hope you enjoy your stitching as much as I have loved designing all the motifs.

Garden sampler
11.6 x 20.6cm
(4½ x 20⅛ in)

Worked on 14-count fabric.

Following a theme, lovely sampler designs can be made by mixing and matching motifs (see page 15).

Materials

You do not need many materials to start cross stitching – just threads, fabric, needles, scissors and a good frame, plus your project requirements. Do buy good-quality threads and fabrics for special pieces. This embroidery technique can be addictive, but even if this is the case, the expense is minimal.

Threads

Embroidery threads consist of six single strands that are twisted together, and these can be split depending on the count of the fabric you are using. I prefer to use DMC threads because the colour range and quality are excellent. The DMC standard cotton thread is the most popular choice for cross stitch, and you may also like using their satin thread, which is gorgeous if you want to add a rich, silky finish to your design. I love their glow-in-the-dark threads from the Light Effects range too, which are perfect for a Halloween or Christmas project. If your motifs are going to be applied to items that will require washing, do make sure that your threads are colourfast before starting to stitch. Test a small sample first.

Needles

The best needles to use for cross stitch are the blunt tapestry needles because they slide in and out of the evenweave fabric smoothly, and the best are sizes 22, 24, 26 and 28. The higher the number, the finer your needle will be.

Scissors

Embroidery scissors are small and sharp with pointed ends. Never cut paper with them as they will become blunt very quickly.

Opposite: stranded embroidery threads, tapestry needles and embroidery scissors.

Fabrics

Cross stitch is described as a counted-thread technique, because it is normally worked on an evenweave fabric or Aida.

In every 2.5cm (1in) of evenweave fabric, there are the same number of warp and weft threads. This offers a grid structure across and down, making it an ideal fabric for cross stitch. It is available in a variety of colours, in 22, 25, 27, 28 and 32 count grades. Stitching is normally worked over two threads, unlike Aida which is worked over one. The number of threads vary depending on the thread weights and the number is referred to as the count.

Aida is the same with different counts, but it is more solid, offering a good base for beginners, or for those seeking to improve their skills. For the motifs in this book use a 14-count fabric, which is perfect for the mini designs.

Soluble Aida dissolves in warm water, which makes it ideal if you want to add motifs to smooth fabrics or those with an uneven weave.

Vinyl Aida is a versatile man-made type of plastic which can be shaped, folded and cut. It does not fray, is water resistant, and it is ideal for bookmarks, placemats, napkin rings, Christmas decorations, photograph frames and gift tags.

Magic Aida has a printed ten-stitch grid, which makes counting much easier when working. The grid, when immersed in water at a temperature of forty degrees centigrade, will magically disappear.

Plastic canvas is also available in several counts and colours. This can be stitched, then cut to create three-dimensional items.

Aida fabrics, linen evenweave and plastic canvas.

Aida bands are available in several colours, and in a variety of widths and different counts. They can be used as borders on soft furnishings and for small projects.

Frames

Frames or hoops prevent the stitching from being pulled out of shape and they are available in various sizes. While stitching, the fabric can be moved around easily in a hoop to enable you to work on new areas, whereas with a frame this is not possible because the fabric is securely attached to the surrounding wooden bars.

A rectangular frame and hoops.

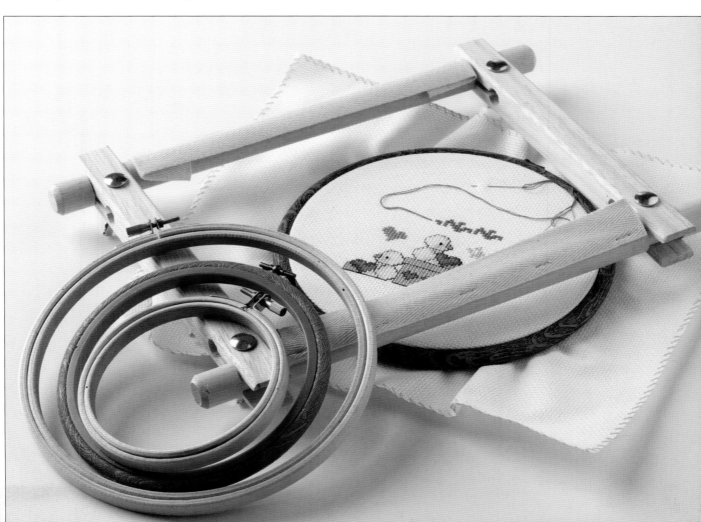

How to Start

This section looks at how to prepare the fabric, how to frame a working piece before beginning your project, and how to stitch. Charts are included throughout the book and are in colour, which makes them clear and easy to follow. Cross stitch is a simple technique and great designs can be stitched easily then used to embellish cards and samplers, or they could be added to clothing, bags, hats and other accessories.

Sizing your design

Knowing the size of your motif is important if you have a particular design in mind. This size will depend on the count of your Aida or evenweave fabric. When working mini motifs I use a 14-count evenweave fabric, which I prefer when stitching smaller designs. You can work out how big or small the finished stitched motif will be by first counting how many squares are in the design across and down. Divide each of the two numbers by the thread count of the fabric. For example, if you are using 14-count Aida, a chart showing 30 x 40 squares should be divided by 14, giving you a design measuring 5.43 x 7.23cm (2.14 x 2.85in).

Preparing the fabric

First decide on the size of the project and cut out the fabric. Always allow plenty of border space around your stitching. For small projects, such as cards, I generally allow 5cm (2in) on all sides, and for larger projects, such as samplers, I allow 10cm (4in). It is much better to have slightly too much border than not enough.

As most fabrics fray, it is a good idea to oversew, or blanket stitch the raw edges before you frame up your work and start to stitch.

It is advisable to find the centre of the design first and to work outwards from there. Simply fold the fabric in half horizontally, then in half again vertically. Where the two folds meet, mark this point with a pin. Unfold the fabric and mark all along the fold lines with tacking stitches, with the stitched lines crossing in the centre. This is where your first stitch will be.

Tip

Oversew raw edges before you frame up your work.

Your chosen design may be a tiny bit smaller than you would like. Adding a small border, even a line of running stitch, can resolve this problem, as shown here.

Framing

For the small motifs in this book you can use a mini frame, or a flexihoop frame, which is either oval, round or square. If your project is larger, for example, if you are stitching a sampler, a bigger rectangular frame can be used.

Using the Charts

If you are using evenweave or Aida fabric, charts are part of the working process. Each block, or set of threads, is a single square on the chart, which represents one complete cross stitch, and the colour of each square shows the thread shade.

Back stitch is shown as a black line around and within the motifs, and each stitch is worked over one block or set of threads.

French knots are represented by dots on the charts, and these are used mainly as eyes on animals and people, but they do occur elsewhere.

Combining motifs

Motifs can be grouped together to create beautiful samplers or designs for a special card or gift. Too many will make your design look cluttered, while too few will give an empty look. Simple planning is the key to creating a good design and getting the right balance will create a stunning result. To combine the motifs, copy them on to graph paper, then cut them out and arrange them on a larger sheet of graph paper. If you want to use the motifs without overlapping, leave two extra squares around each image. If you are going to overlap motifs, cut around the outline edge of the images and carefully lay them over each other. Play with them until you have a layout you are happy with, then secure them in place with glue or sticky tape.

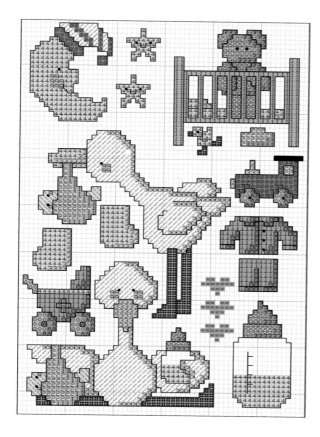

This chart (see page 66), includes all the stitches on the following pages. The cross stitch used on the motifs is embellished with French knots for the characters' eyes, and back stitch tightens up the images, giving them a more solid shape.

Stitches

Cross stitch

Cross stitches can be worked horizontally, vertically and individually in designs.

1 Take an approximate 76.2cm (30in) length of single thread and fold it in half. Thread the two ends through the eye of your needle.

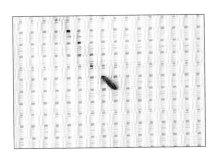

2 Bring the needle up through the fabric and pass it back down diagonally, leaving the loop end at the back of the fabric.

3 Secure your work at the back of the fabric by passing the needle and thread through the loop end.

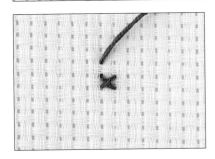

4 On the front of the fabric, work another stitch in the opposite direction, thus creating your first cross stitch.

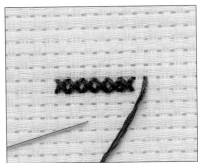

5 Continue to make cross stitches in the same way, making sure that the second half of each cross is always worked in the same direction.

Back stitch

Thread the needle and secure the thread (see steps 1–3 opposite).

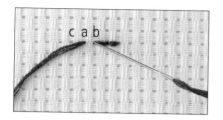 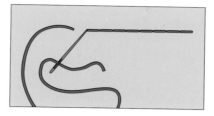

Work from right to left, bringing the needle up through the fabric at (a). Make the stitch by taking the needle down through the fabric at (b), then bring it up two holes along to the left at (c). To continue, pass the needle back down through the left end of the stitch just worked, at (a).

French knot

When working a French knot, I catch a thread of the fabric when winding the embroidery thread around the needle, as this helps to stop the stitch from disappearing to the back.

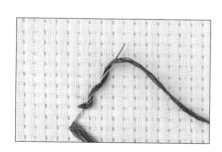

1 Bring the needle up through the fabric and wind the thread twice around the needle.

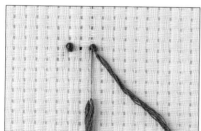

2 Place your fingers on the loops, so that they do not unravel, and pull your needle upwards gently. Pass the needle back through the original hole, ready for your next stitch.

Back stitch

Back stitch can be worked diagonally, as well as horizonatally and vertically.

17

Finishing off

To finish off, thread the needle under a few stitches on the back of your work. Do not pull too tightly as this will distort the stitches. Thread the needle under a few more stitches in a slightly different direction, then snip the thread close to the stitching, with approximately 1cm (⅜ in) spare.

Project Help

Follow any guidelines given when using the stitched pieces in purchased mounts, cards and items. Samplers are lovely as gifts, and motifs can be mixed and matched to create designs for all occasions. Motifs can also be inserted into bought blank aperture cards, and these are available in most craft stores. You can also make bookmarks, key rings and decorative panels, or use the motifs to decorate soft furnishings around the home.

Iron on interfacing

If you are stitching a motif for a key ring, where the back of your work will be visible, it is a good idea to iron a piece of interfacing over the reverse of the stitching when you have finished the design. Not only does this hide any untidy areas, it also helps prevent any fraying that may occur if you have to cut your design to fit your project.

Soluble Aida

Stitched motifs can be attached to many types of fabric, and the easiest method is to use soluble Aida for your project. Select the motif, or motifs, you want to stitch, then calculate the finished size of the design (see page 12).

1. Cut the soluble Aida, 5cm (2in) larger than the finished design.

2. If you are attaching the Aida to smooth, stretch fabric, iron a piece of lightweight interfacing, the same size as the Aida, on to the back of the fabric, where you want to place the motif(s).

3. Pin or tack the Aida to the front of the fabric.

4. Sew it on using slip stitch and a needle with a sharp point.

5. Stitch the motifs, and when you have completed everything, simply leave the embellished fabric in a bowl of warm water at a temperature of 40 °C, for at least ten minutes. The soluble Aida will disintegrate like magic, leaving you with a perfect design on your fabric. Dry and press.

Aftercare

Use colourfast threads if you are planning to wash your stitched motif, for example, if it is going to be used to embellish garments or accessories. To press your work, lay the back of the stitching face up on a soft towel, and gently iron.

Projects

Mini motifs can be applied easily and glued into cards, tags and mounts as shown opposite, or they can be added to garments and accessories. If you choose to do the latter, iron a piece of lightweight interfacing on to the back of the stitched design and, using cotton thread that matches the colour of your evenweave fabric, oversew the edges of the motif to prevent fraying, then stitch it in place.

The Motifs

These mix- and -match motifs are grouped into
popular subjects, from the cute and loveable
animals opposite right through to the zodiac series.
The thread colours and related symbols on the
charts are shown on page 254, and a helpful index
on the final pages of the book lists all the characters
in this fun collection.

This sampler uses motifs from pages 55–67

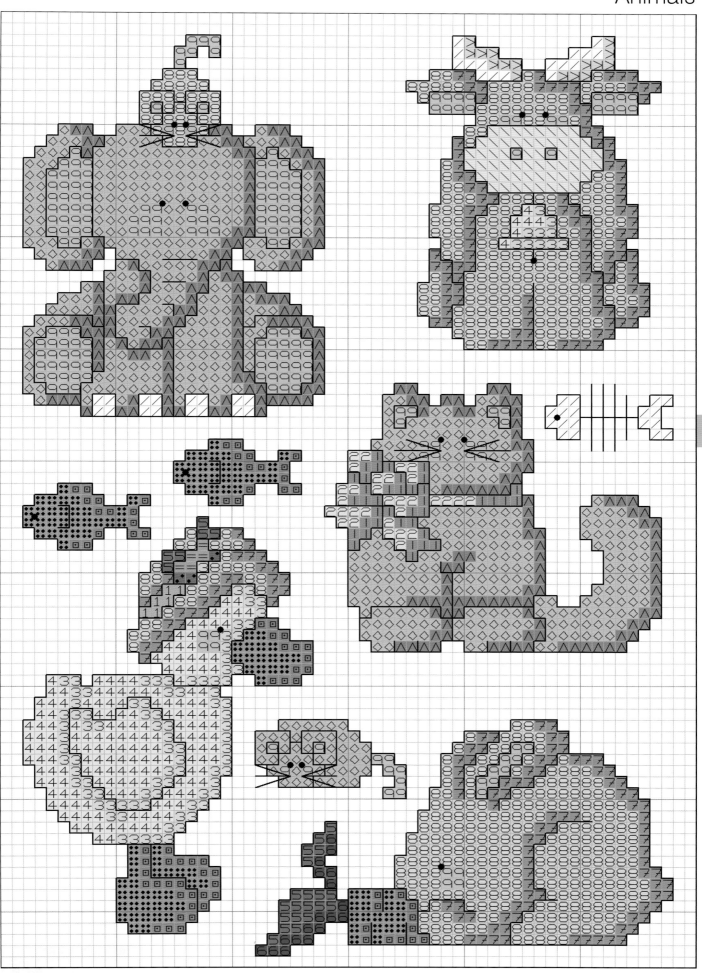

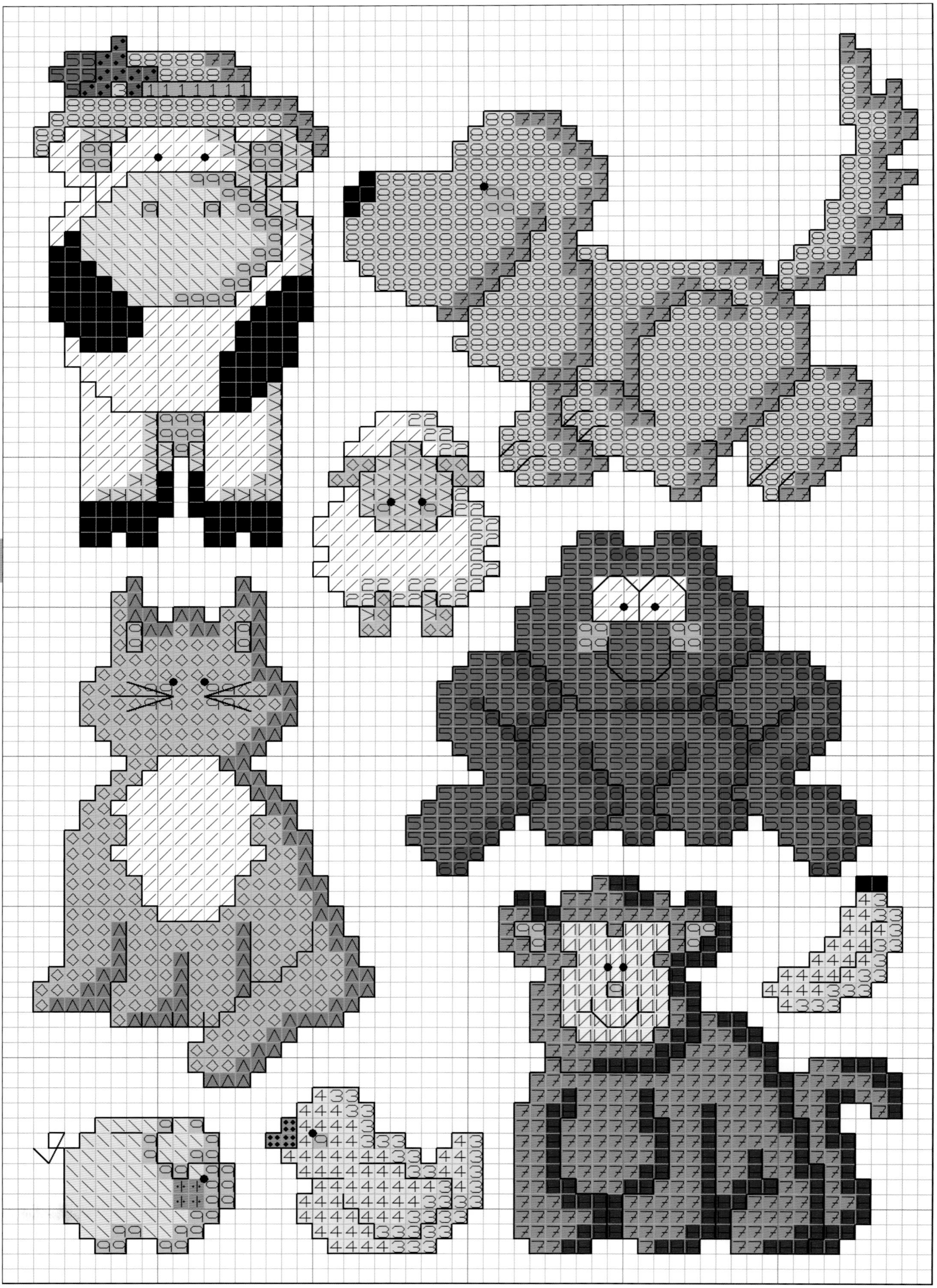

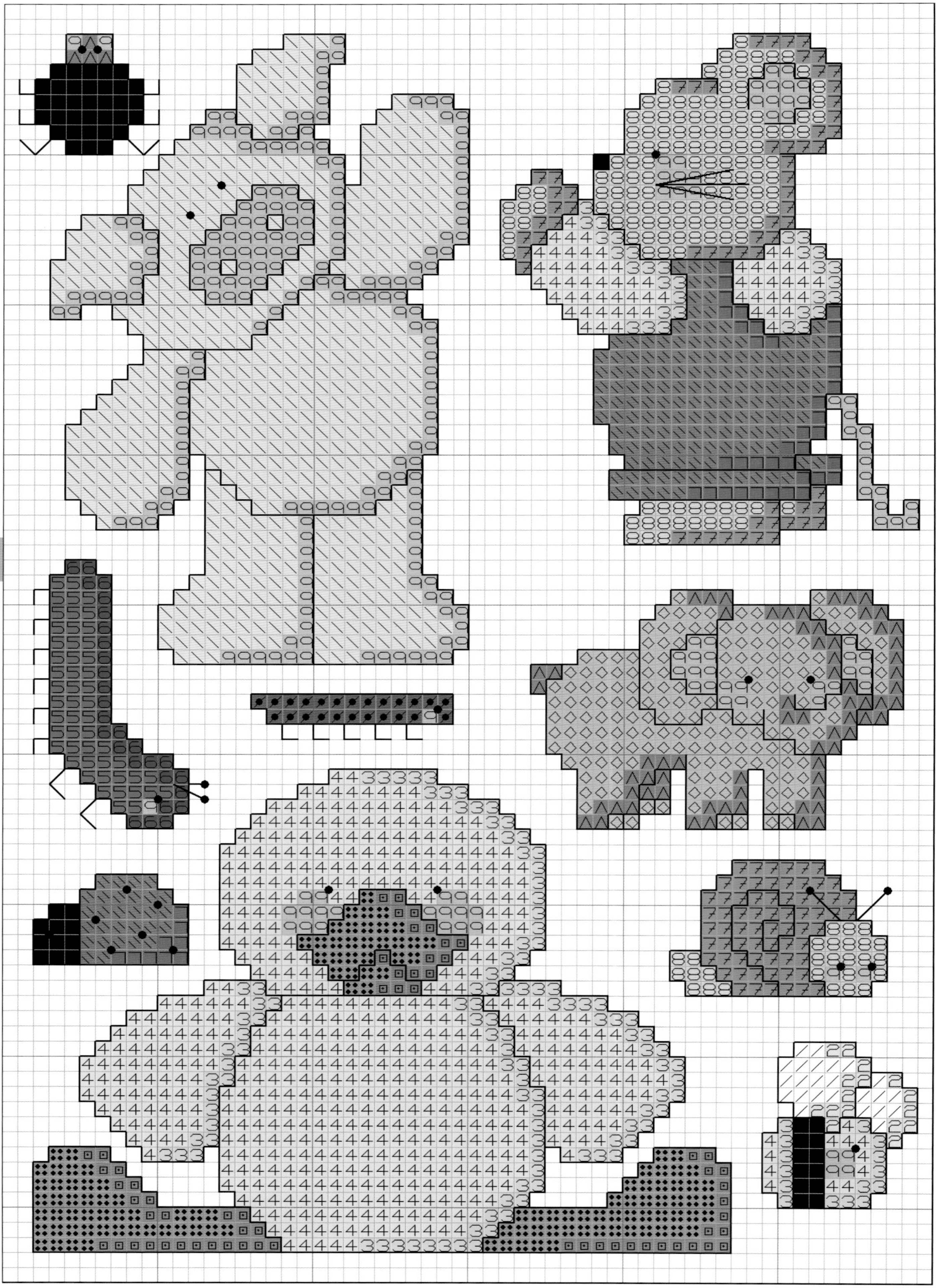

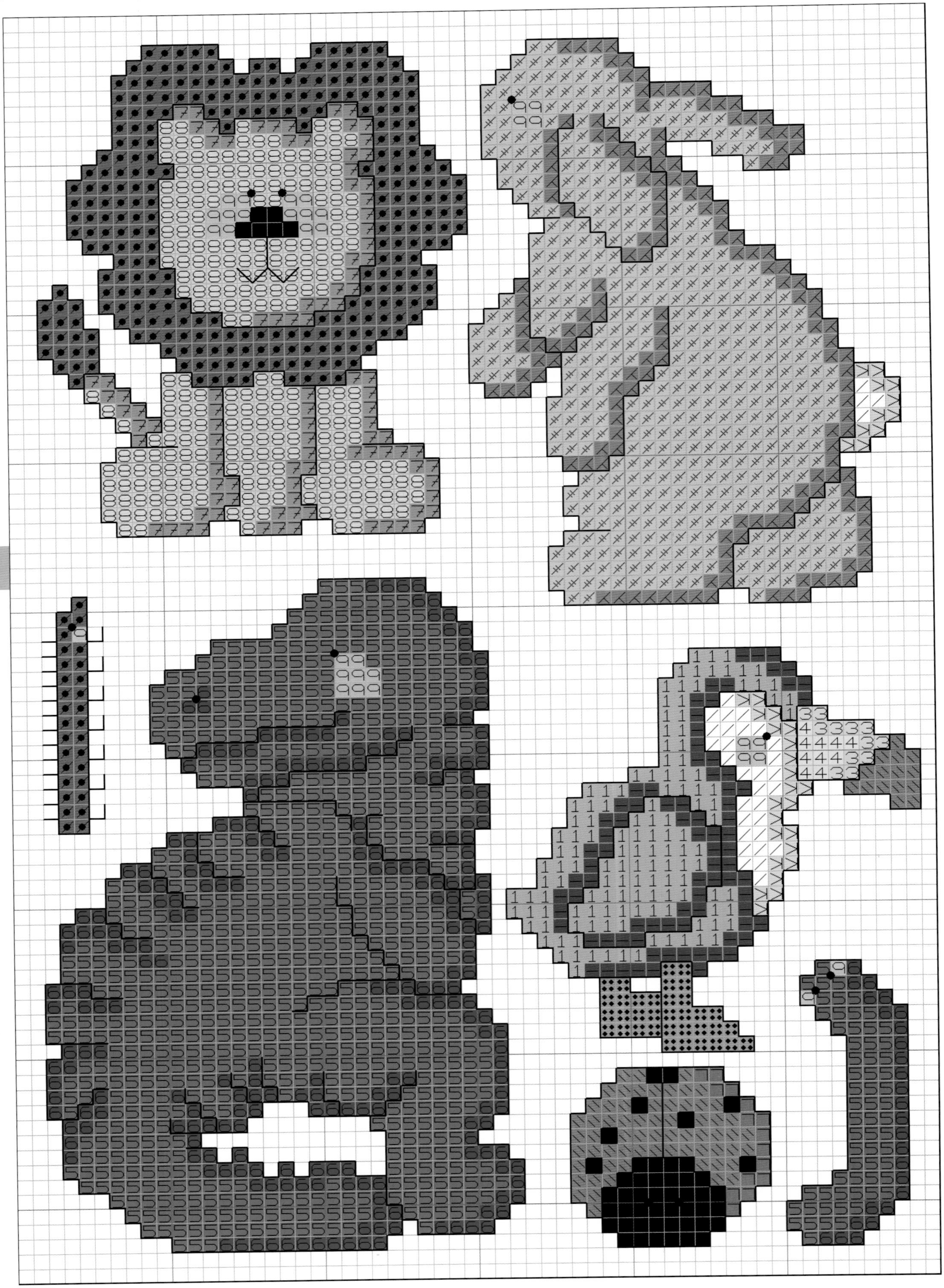

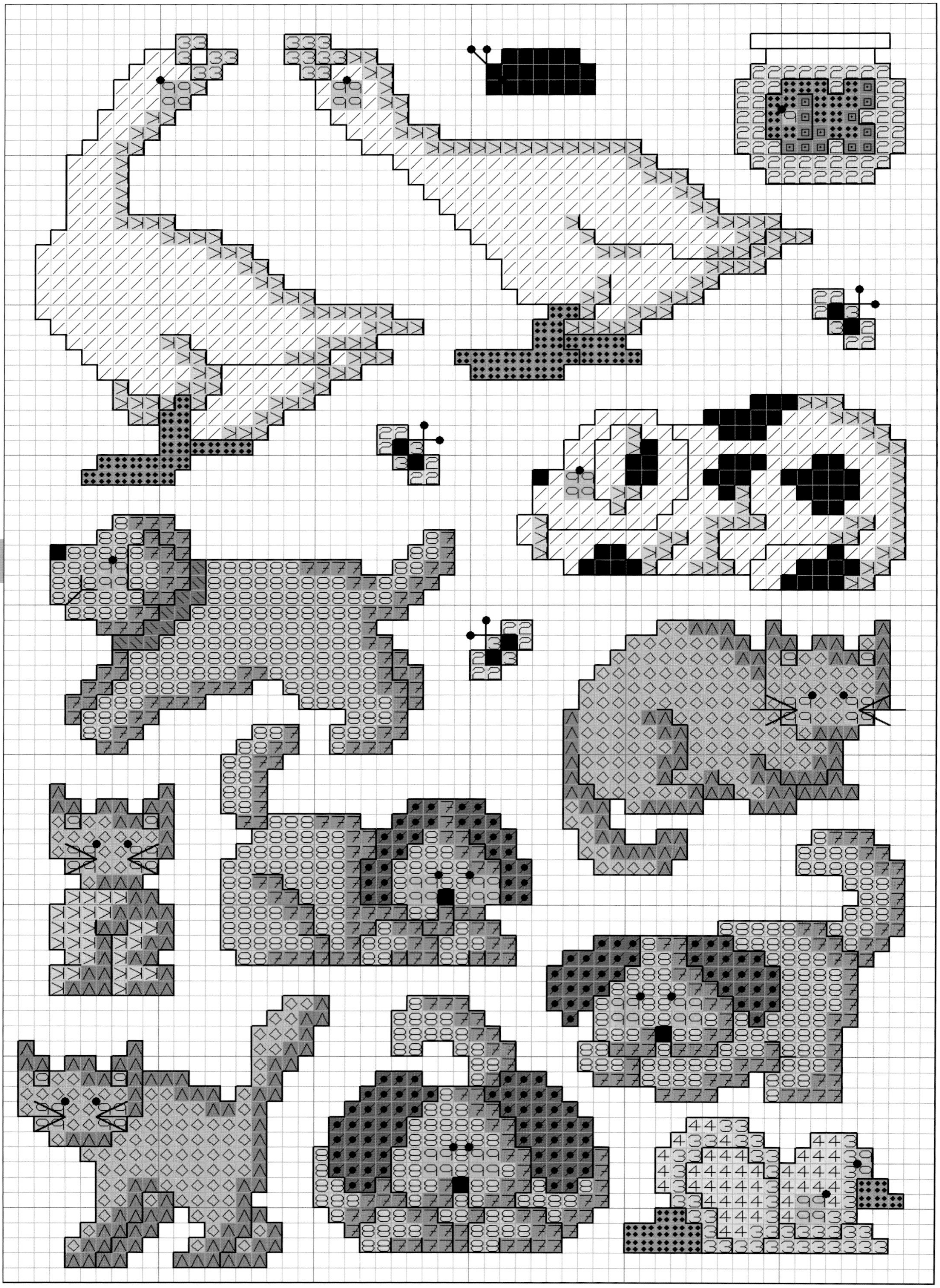

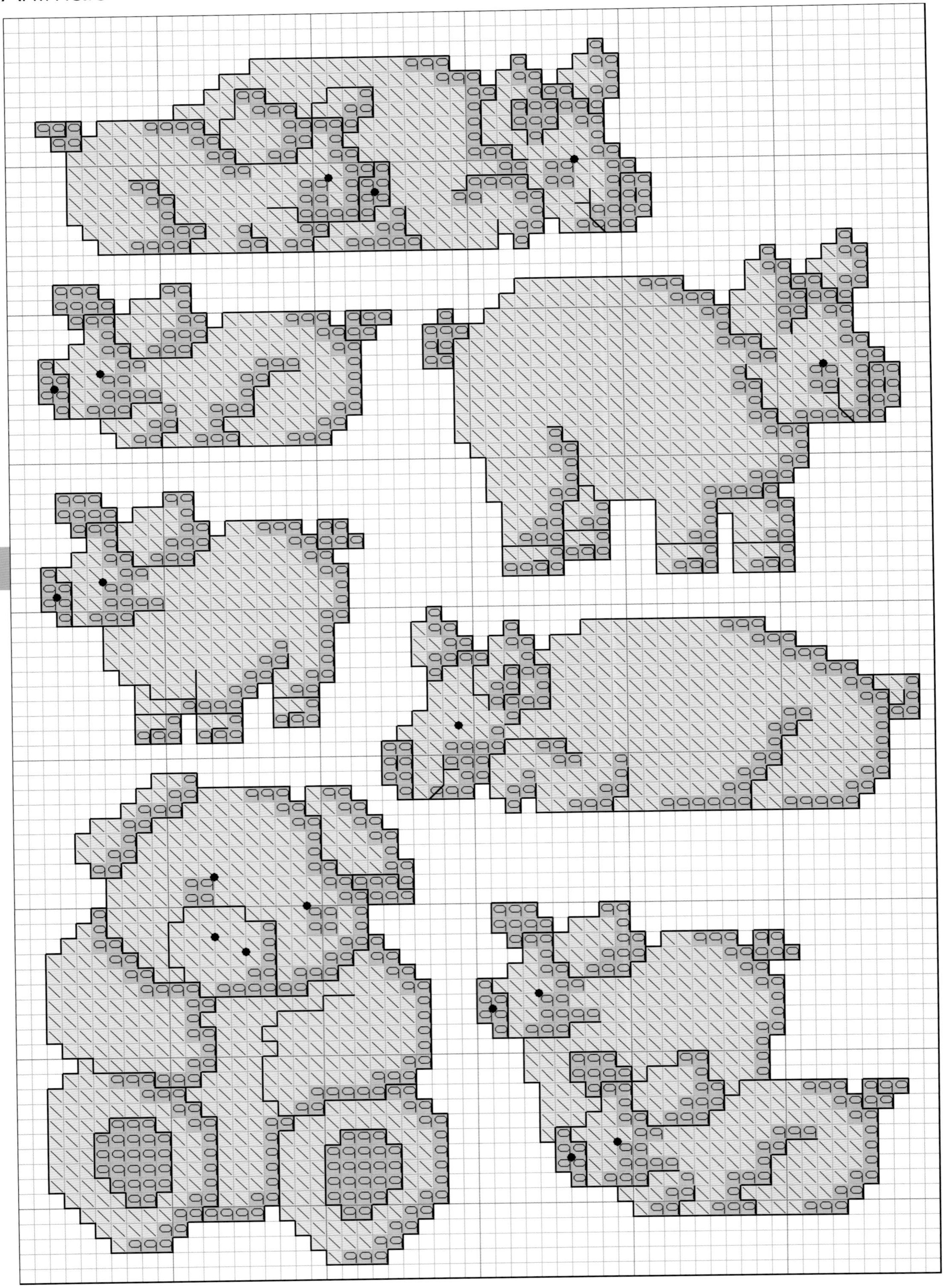

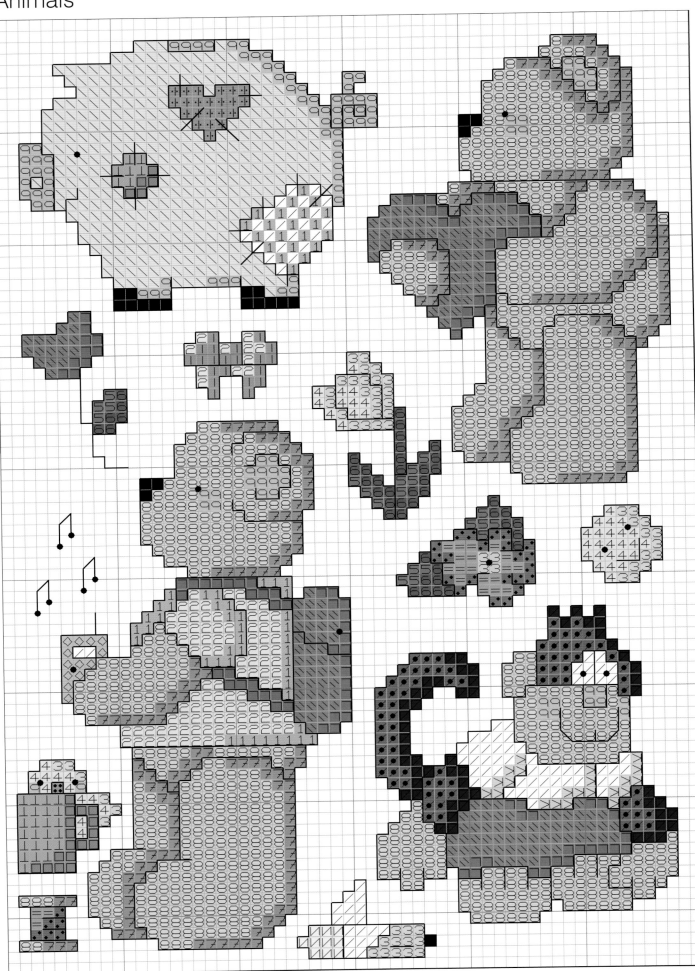

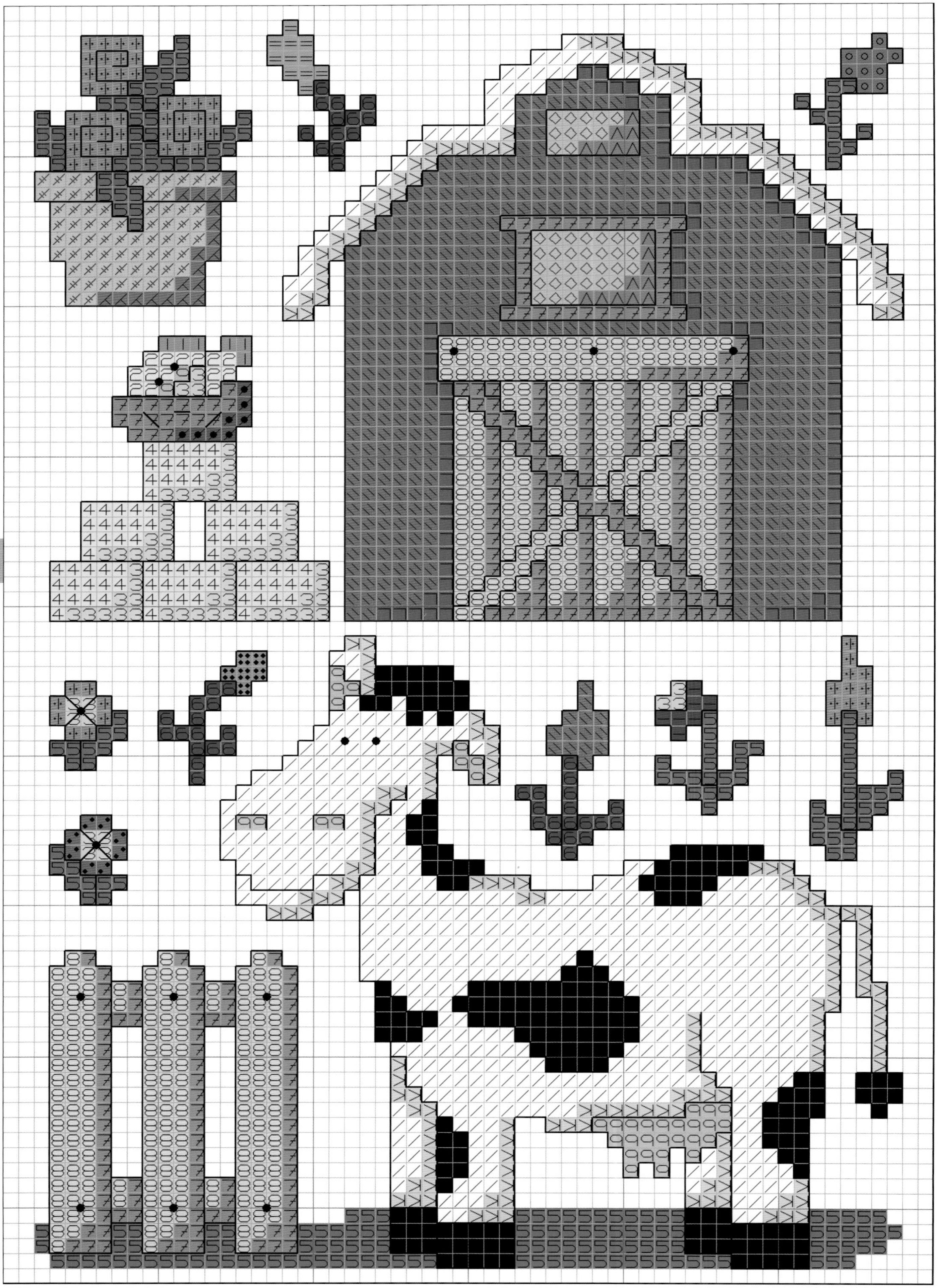

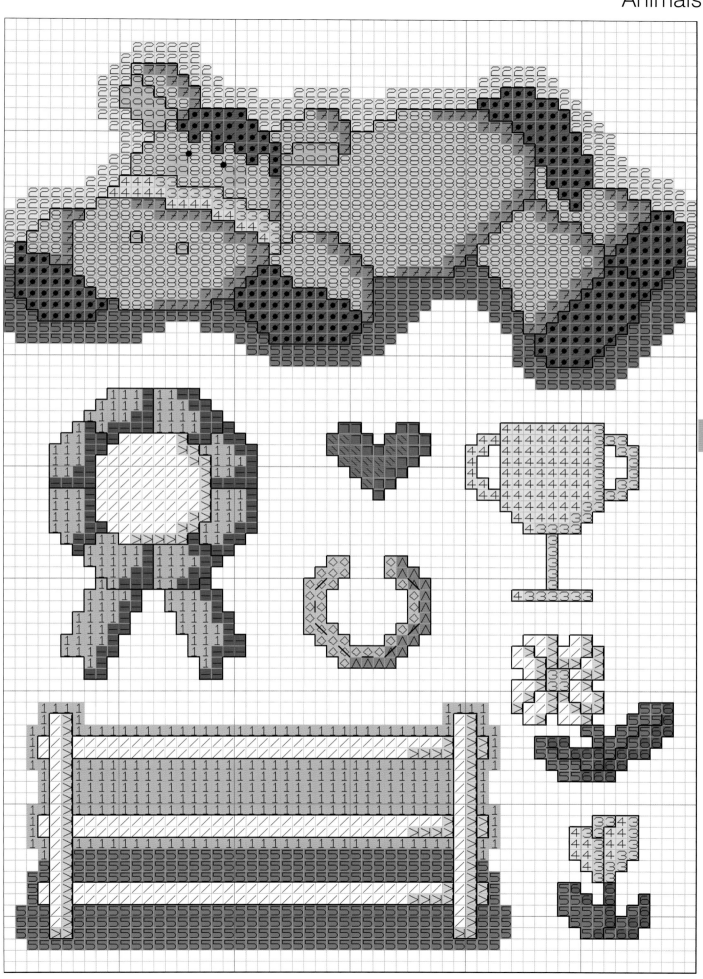

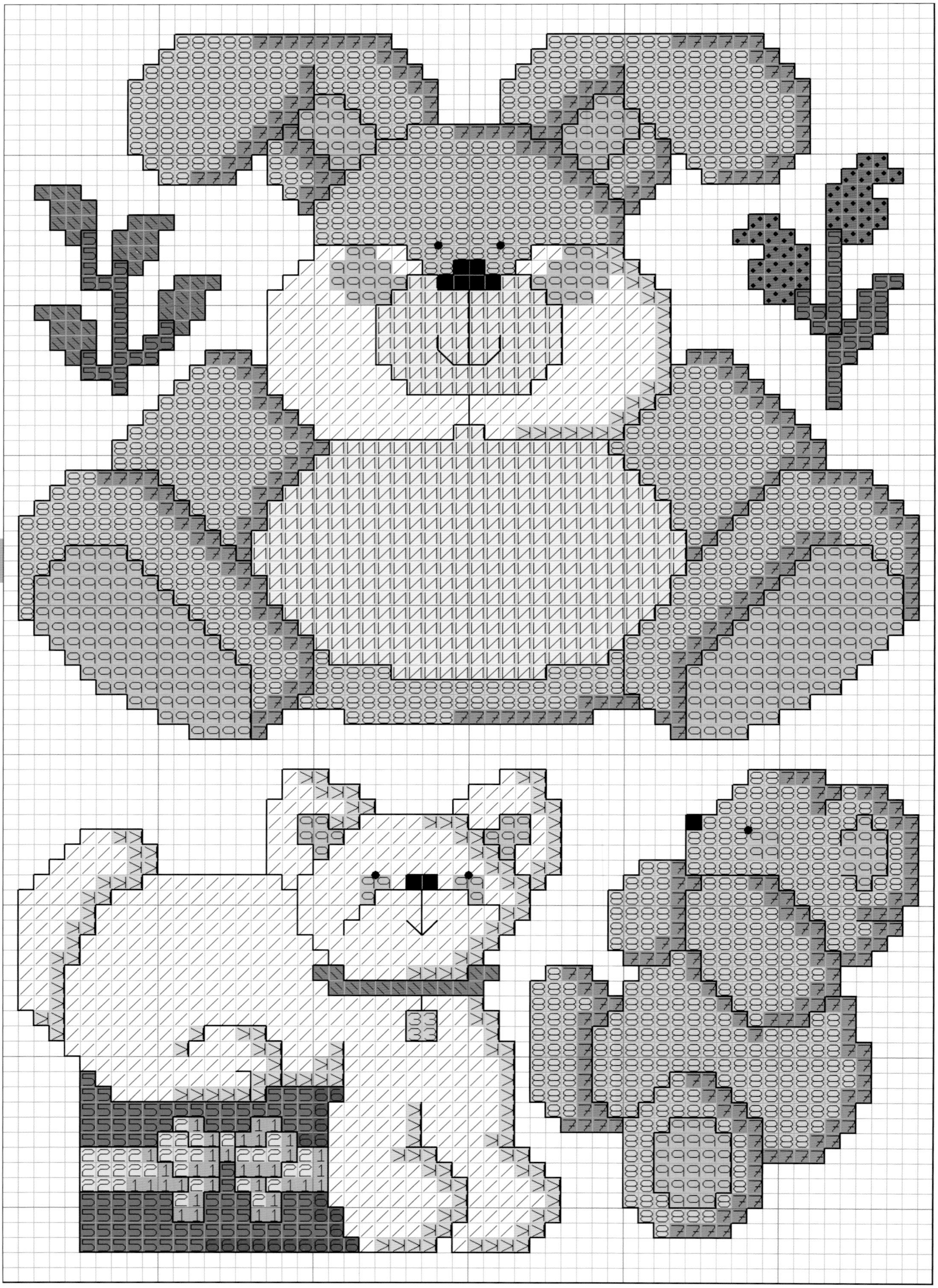

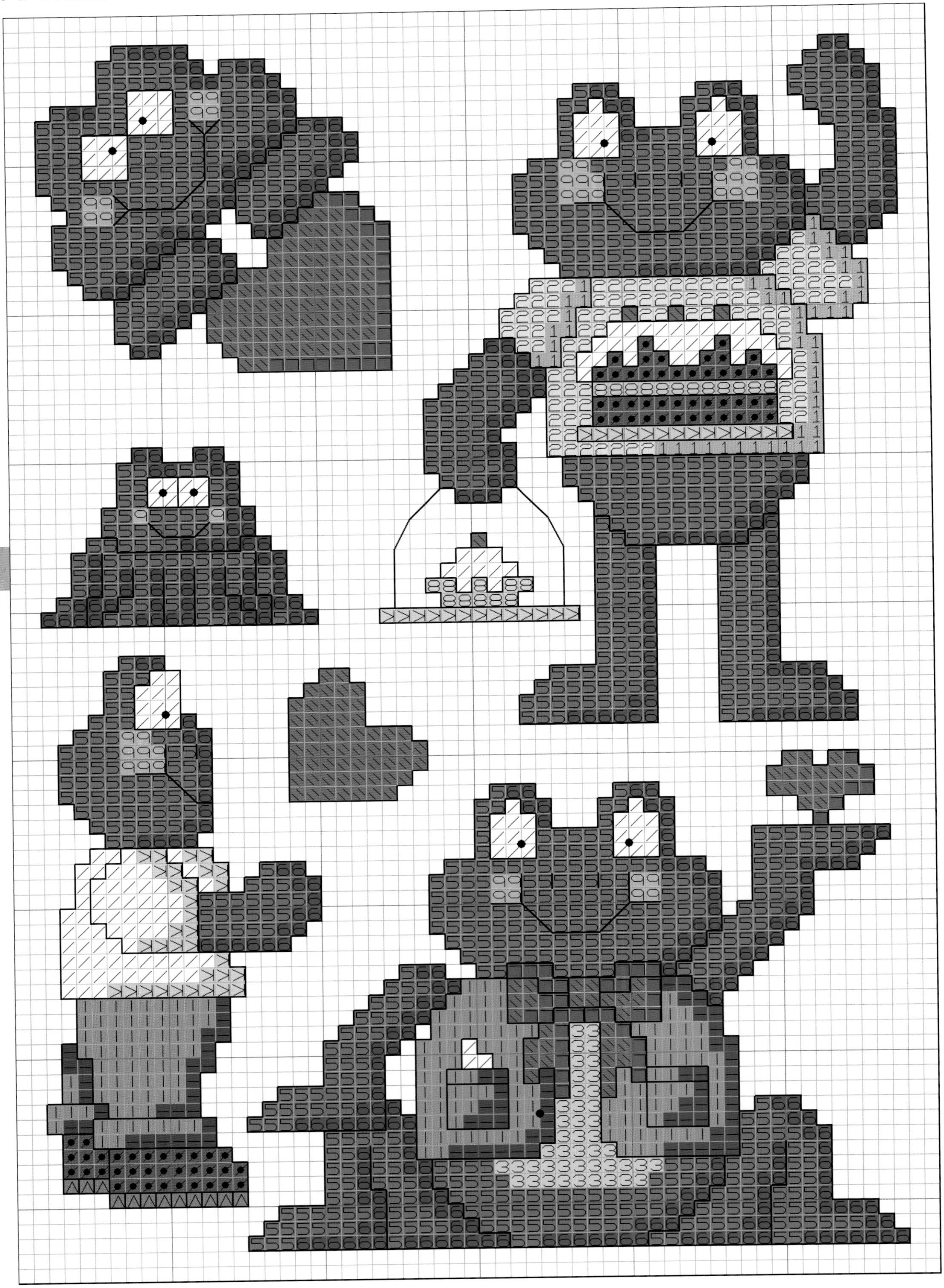

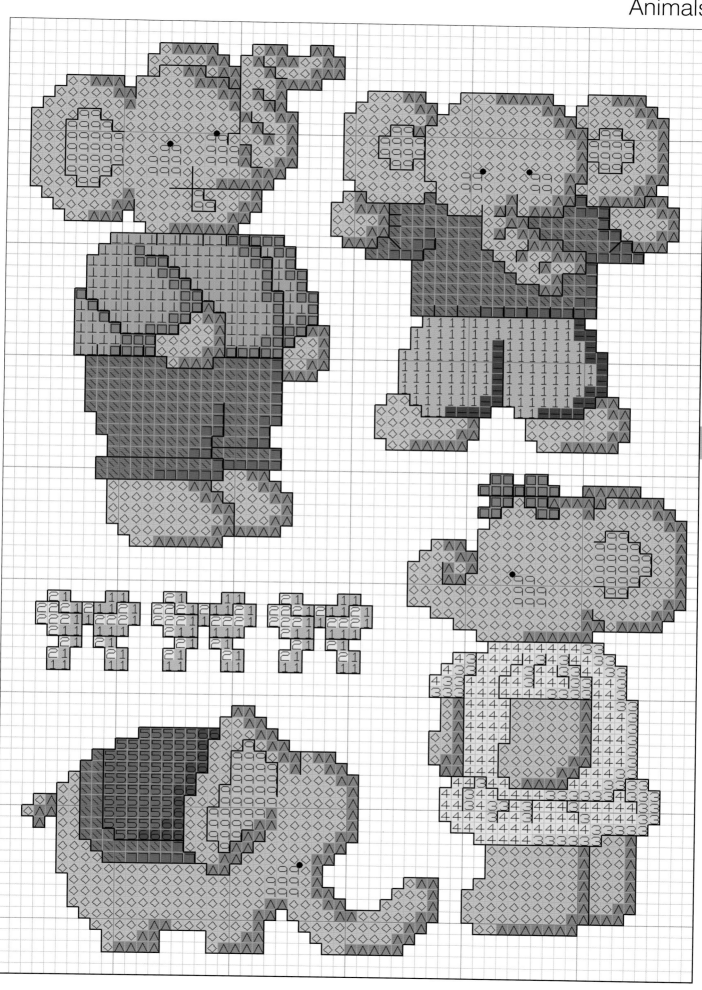

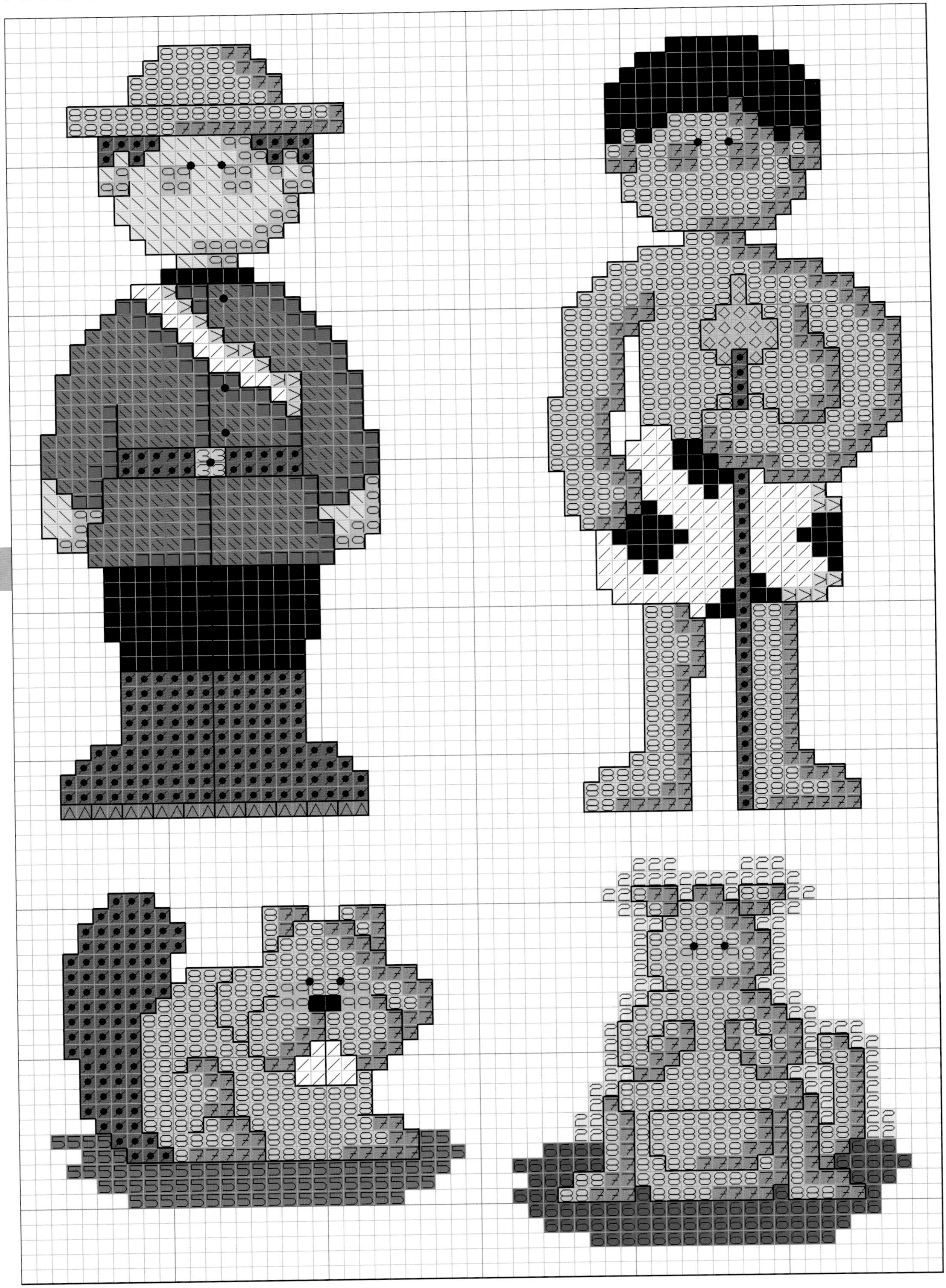

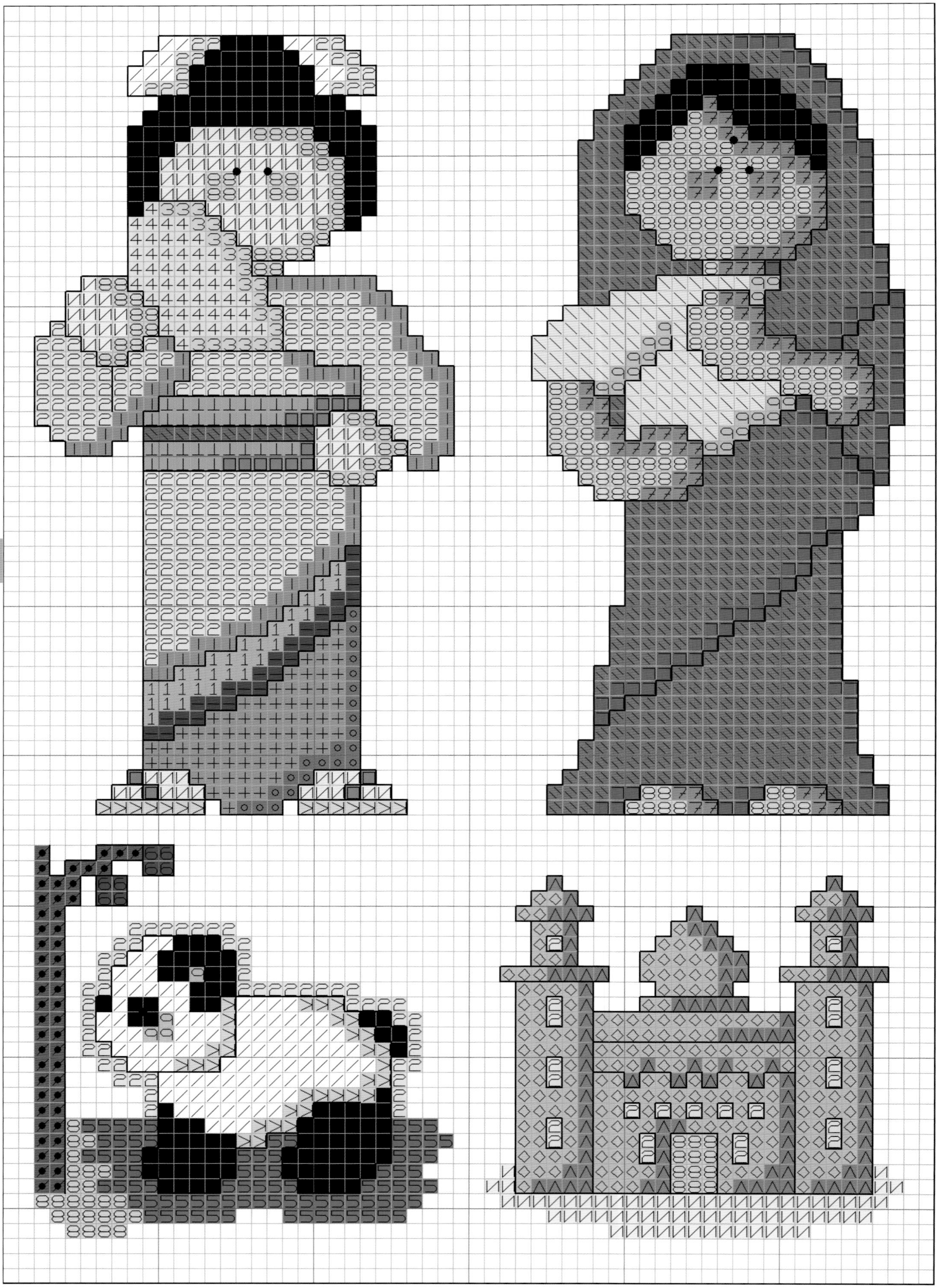

44

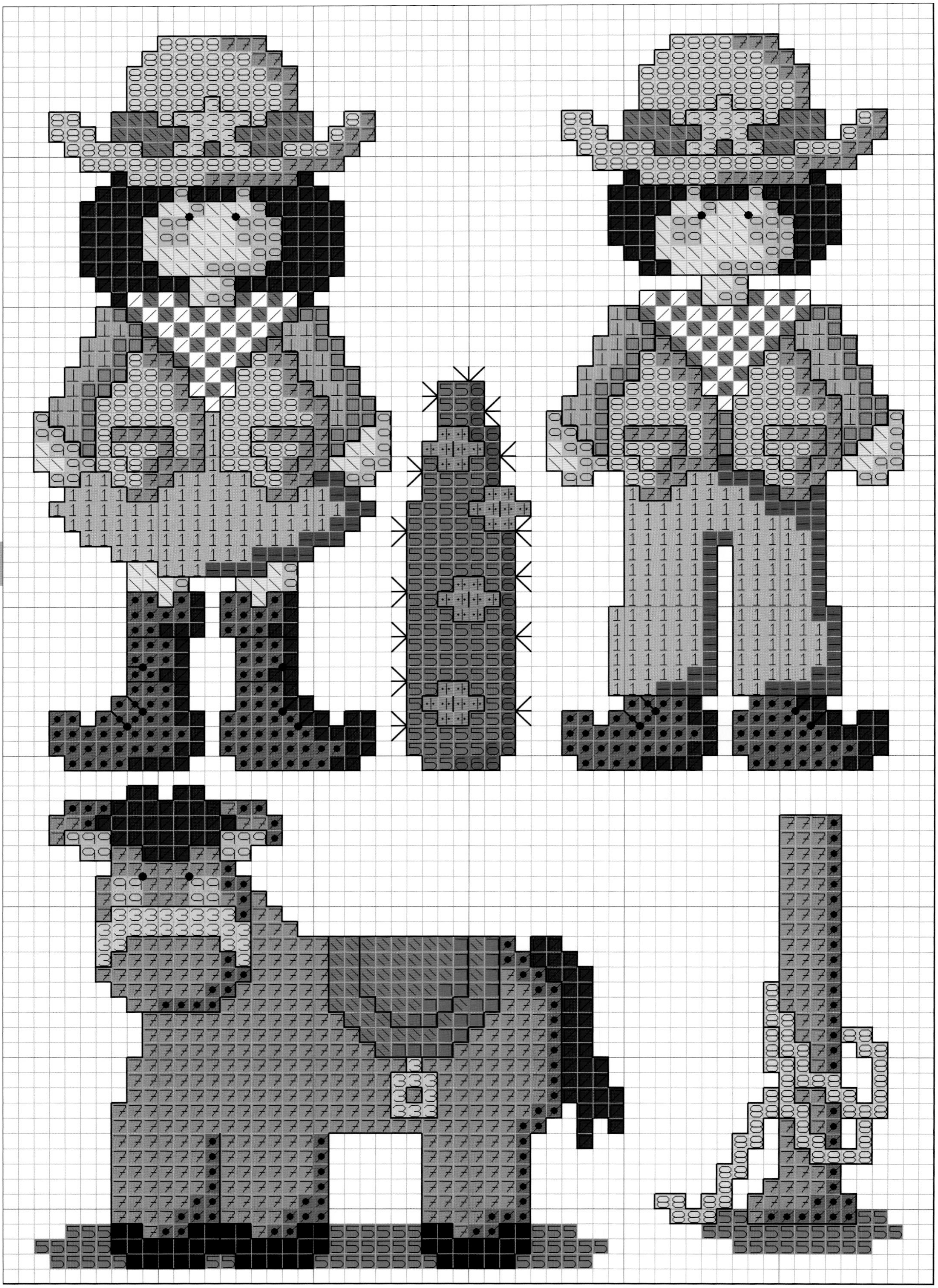

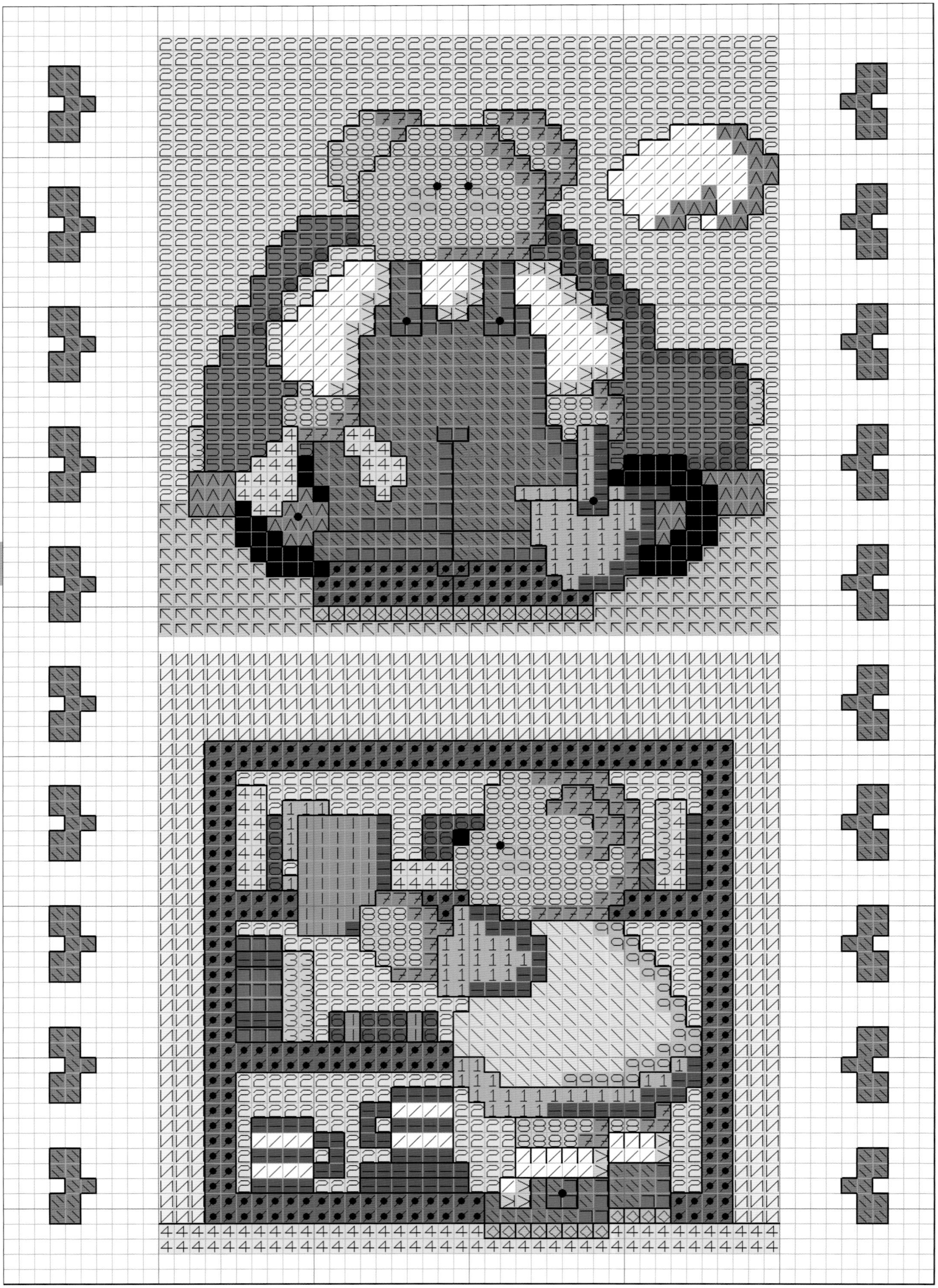

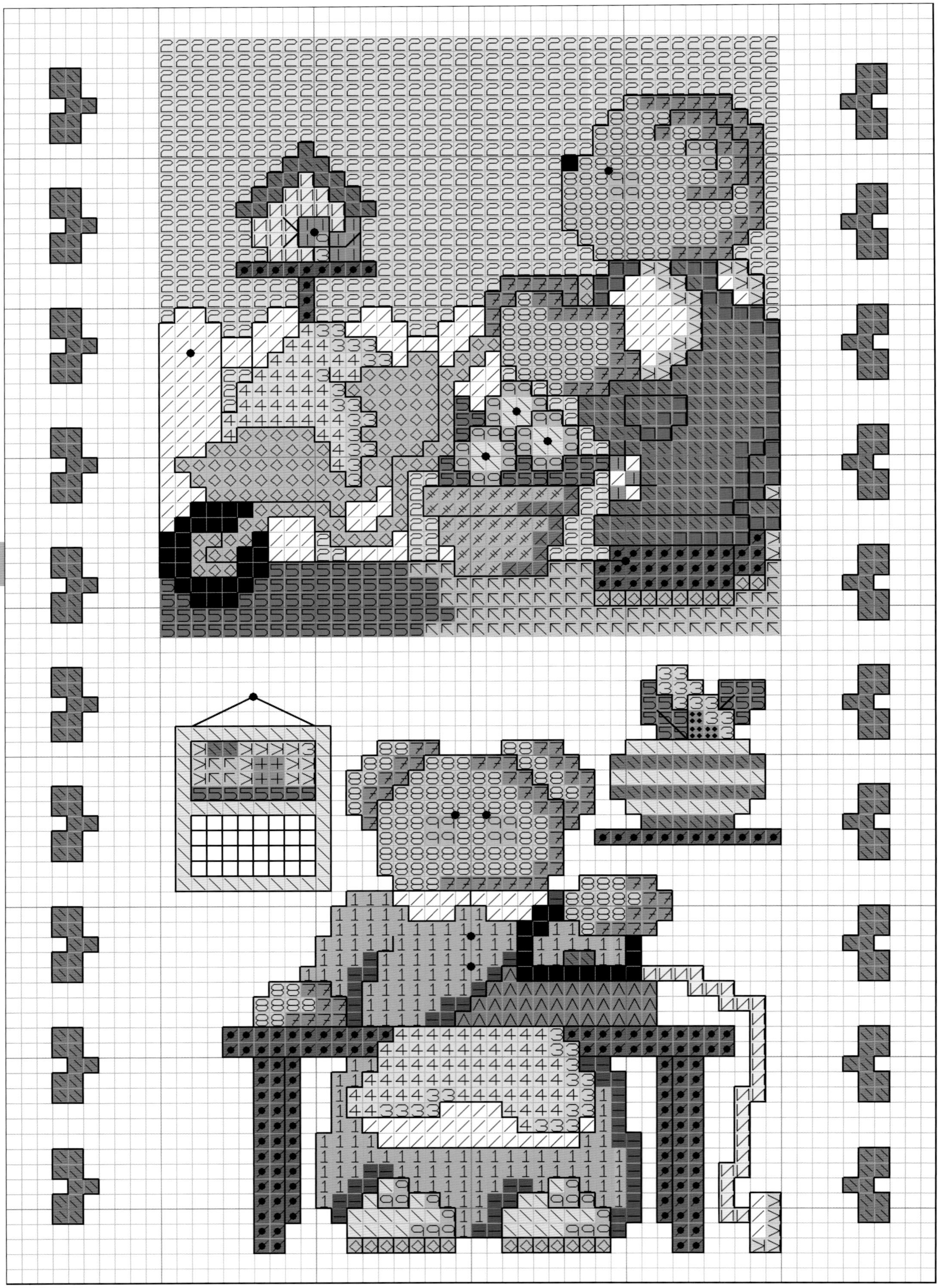

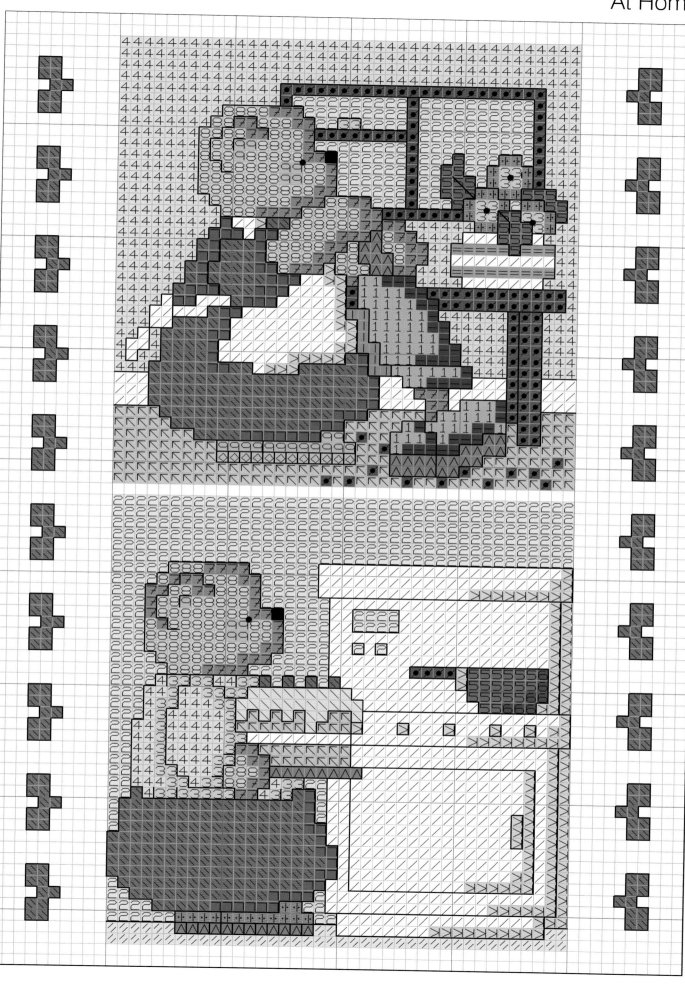

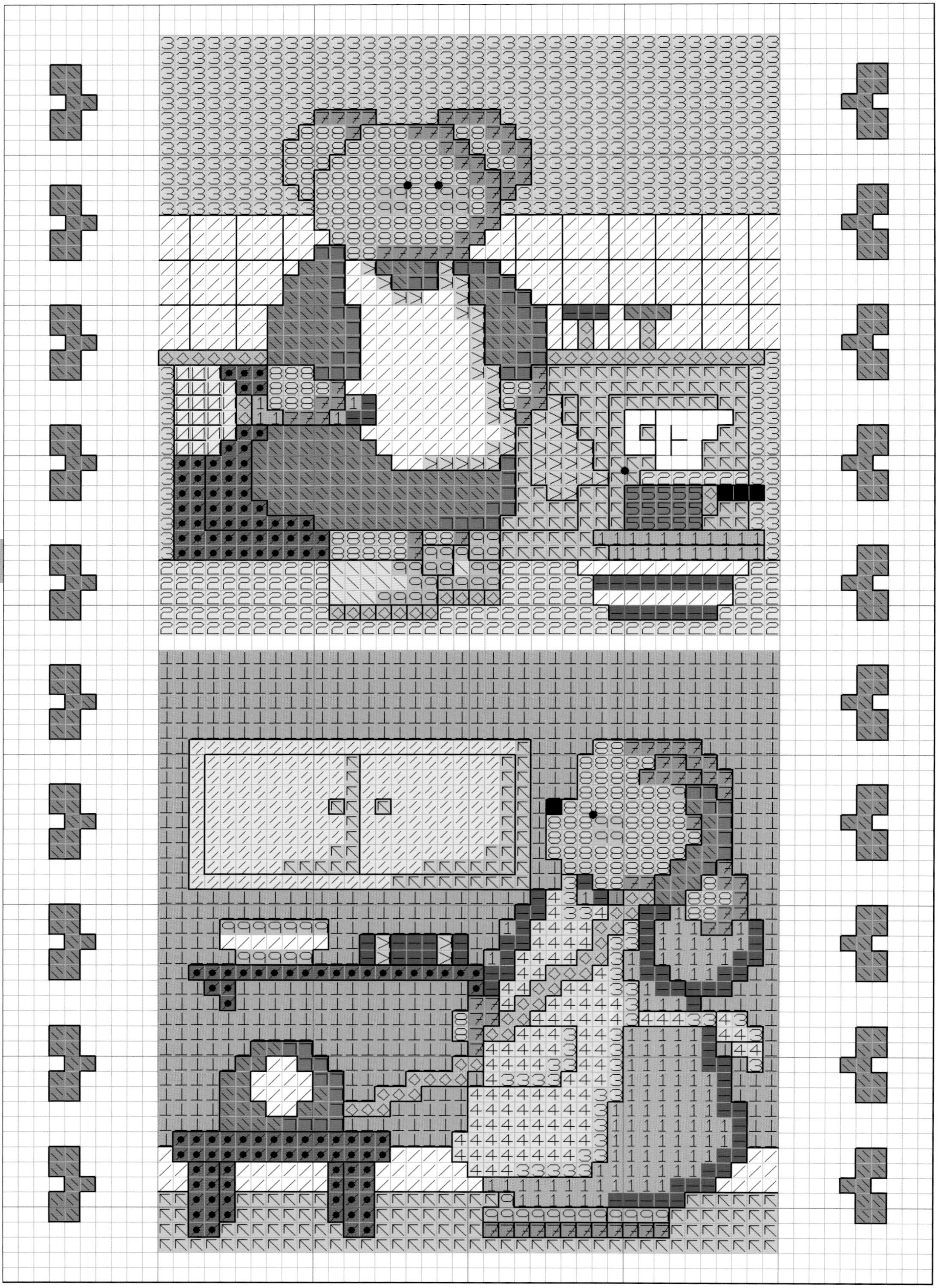

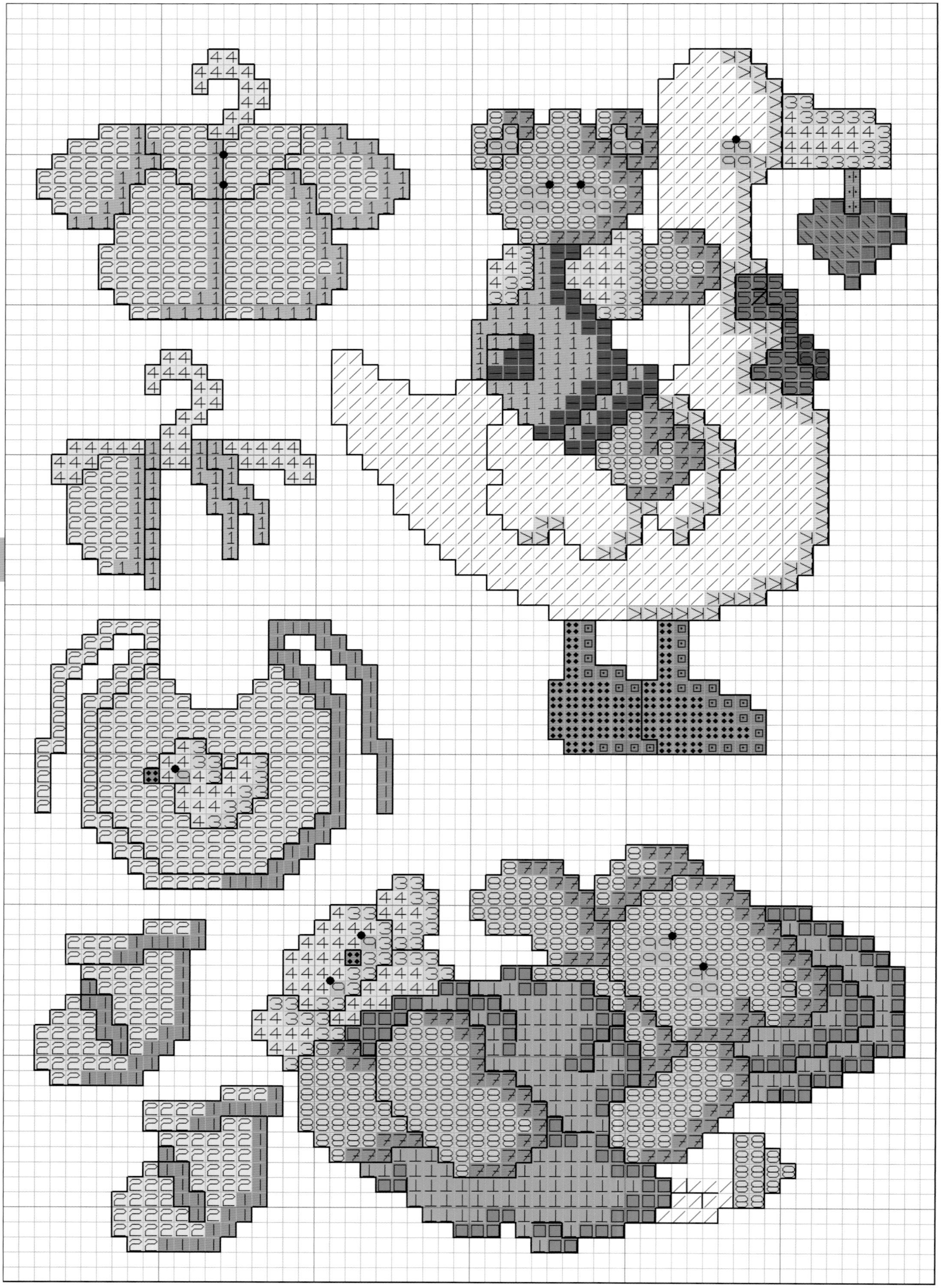

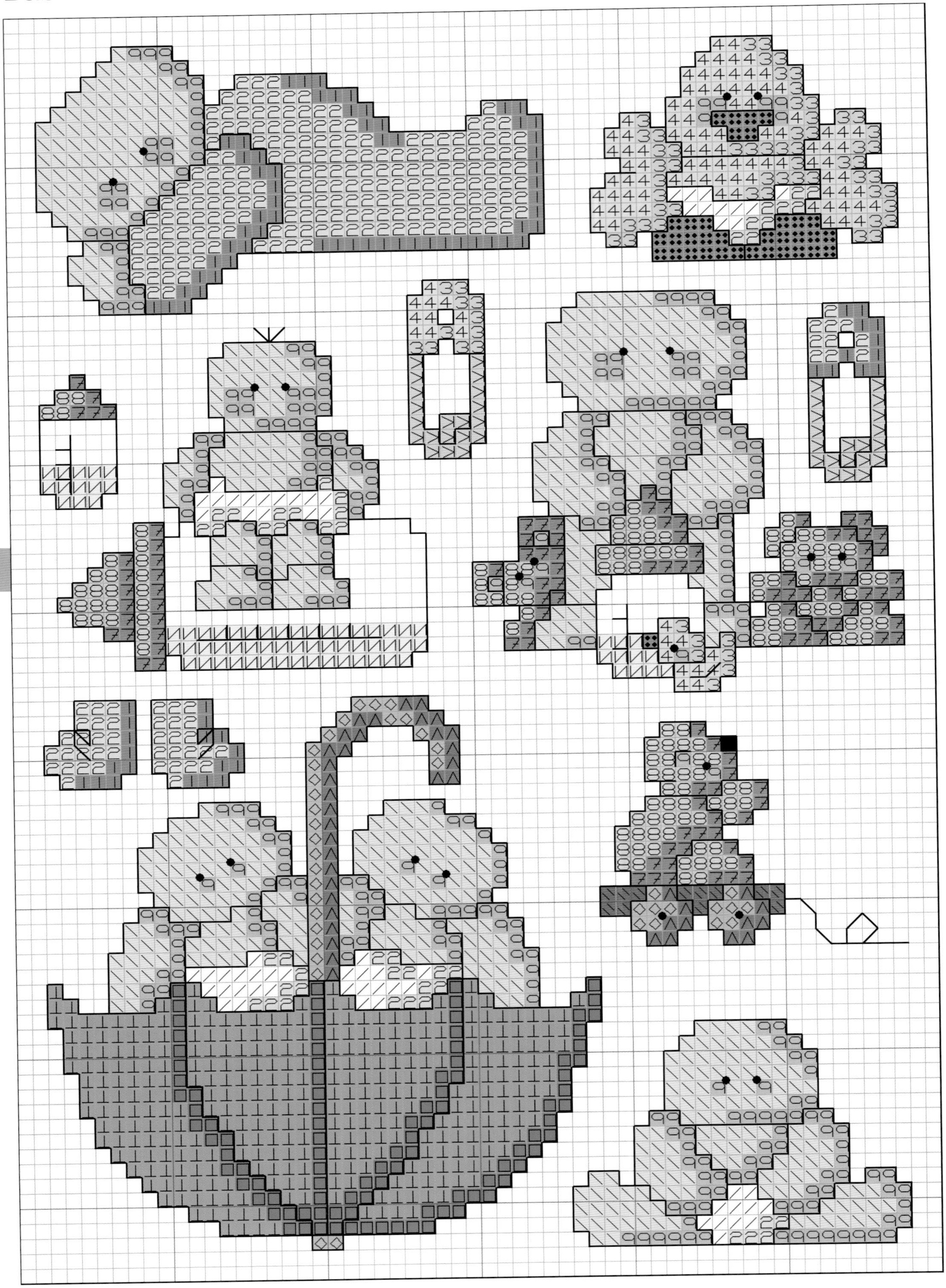

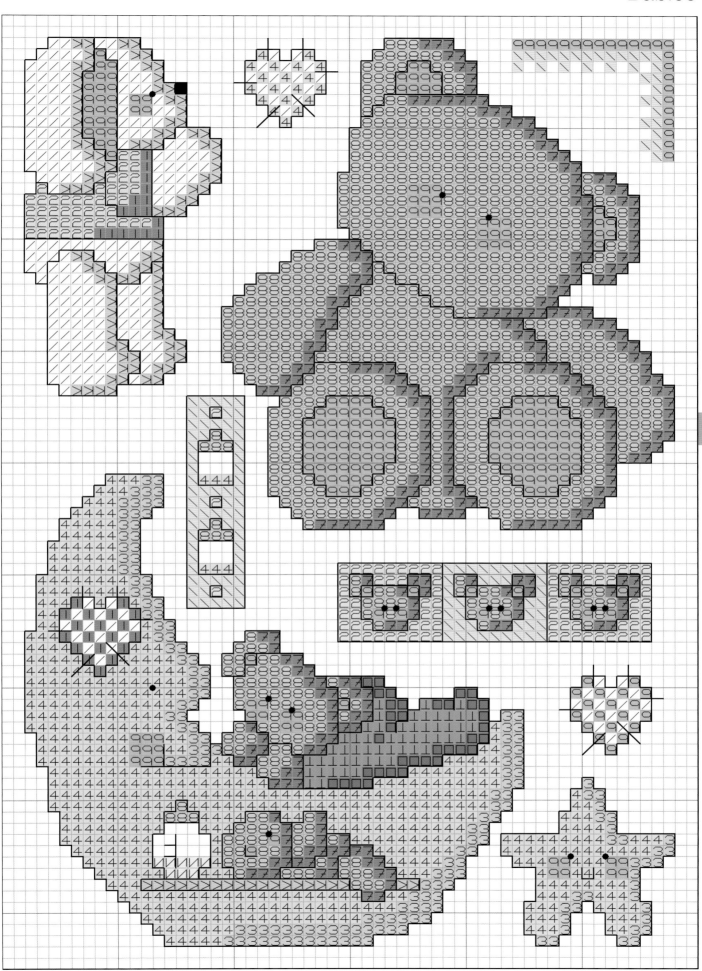

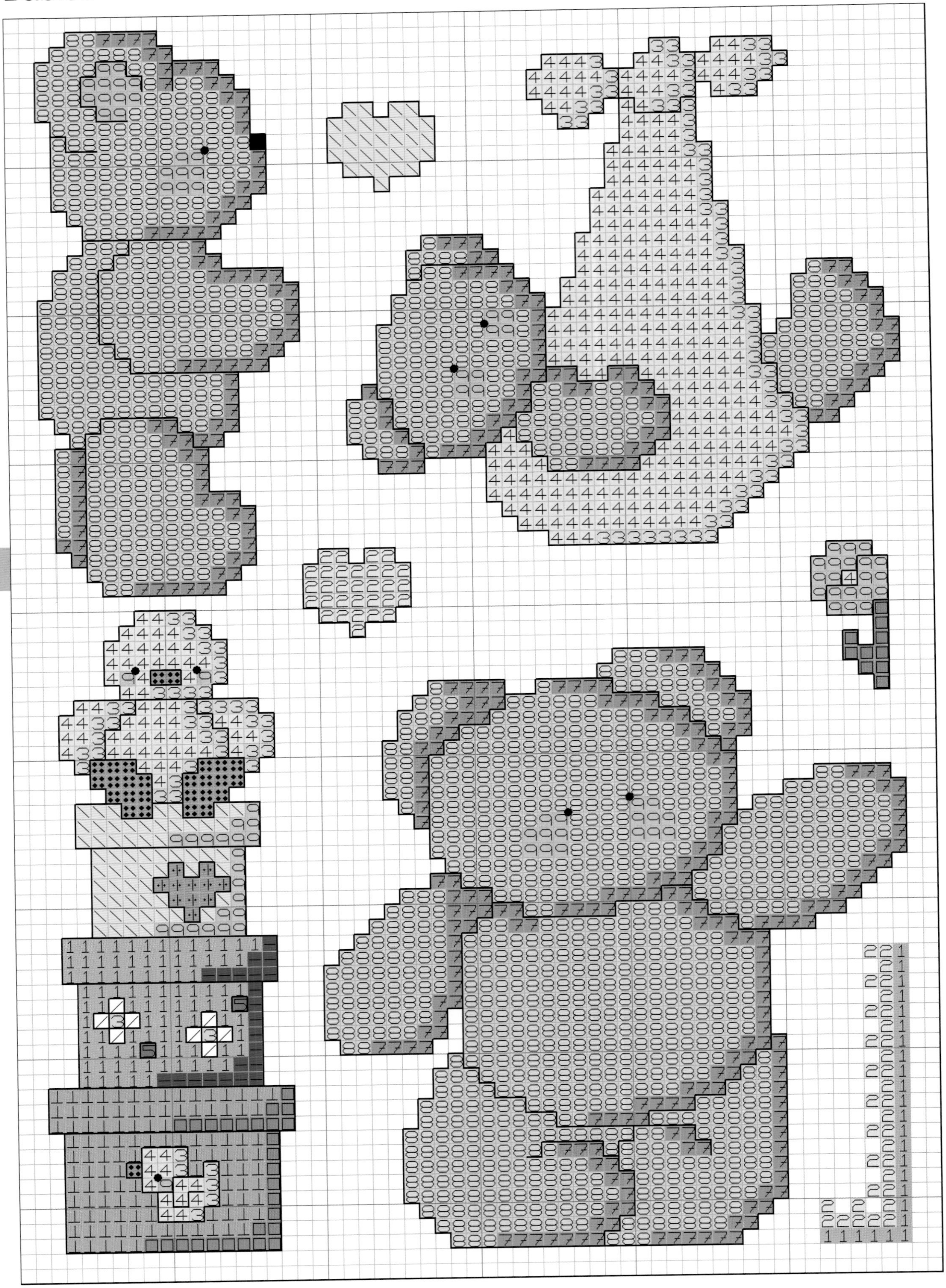

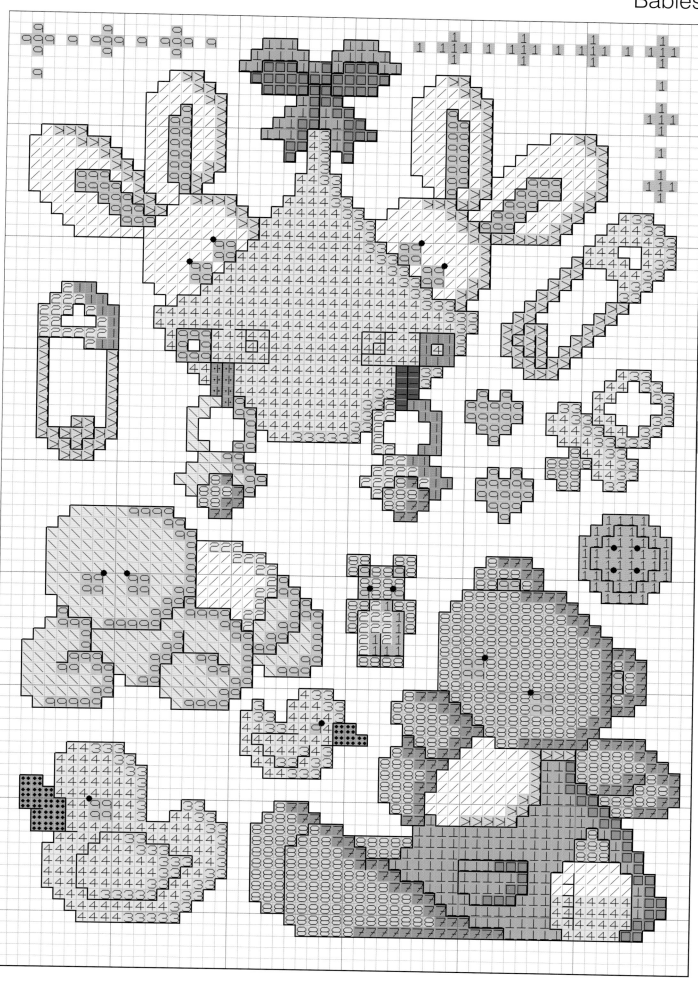

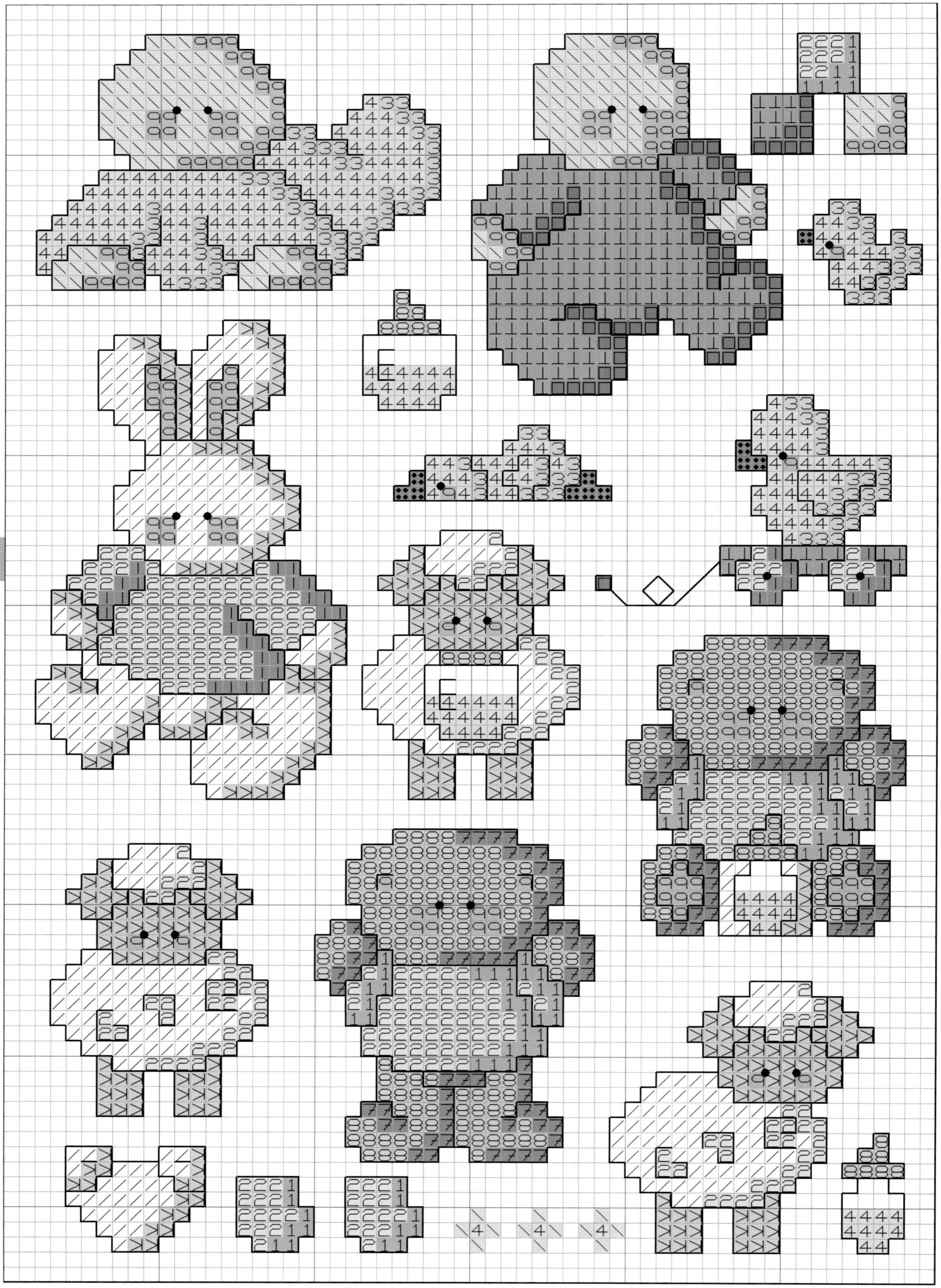

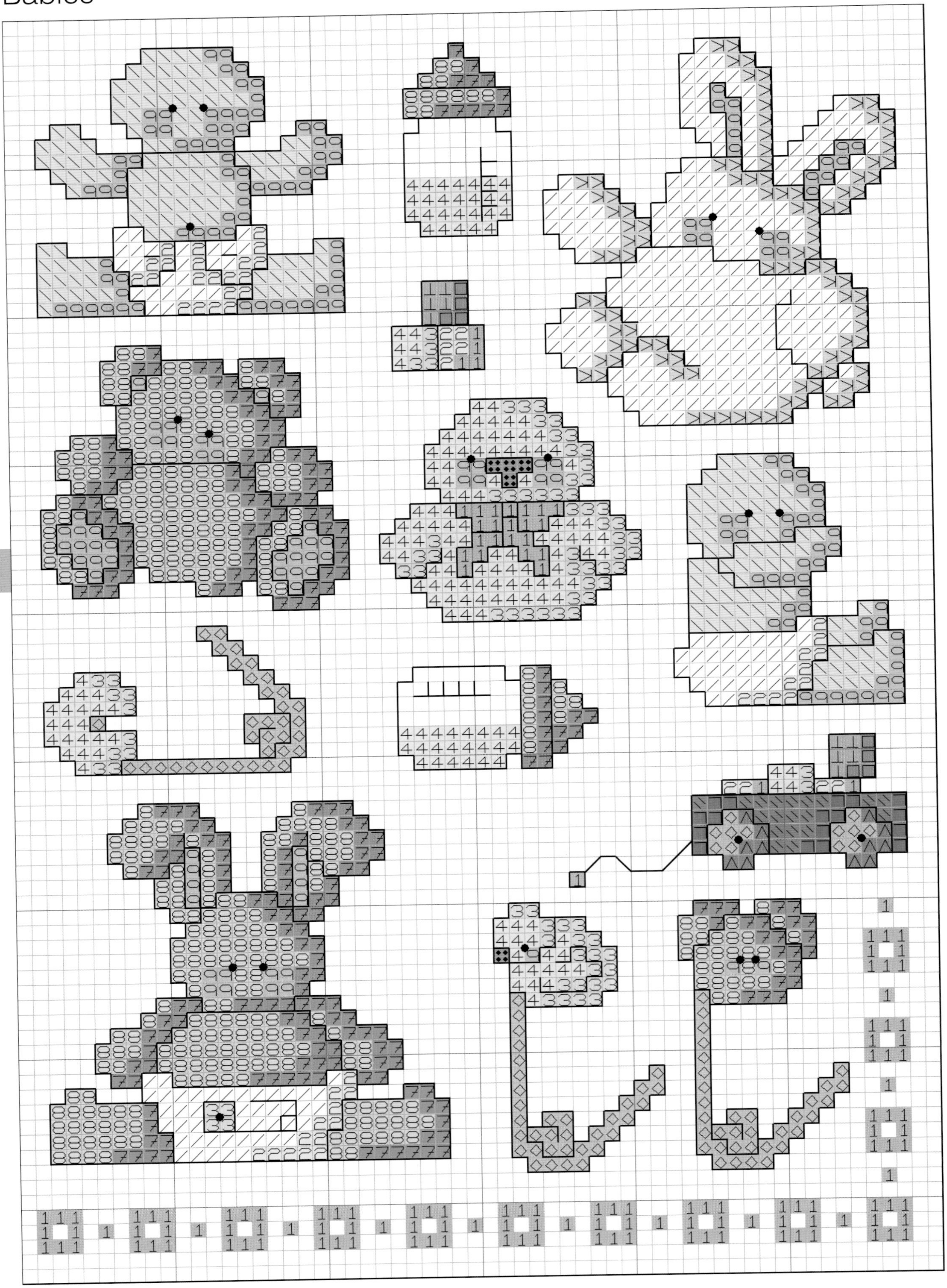

Babies

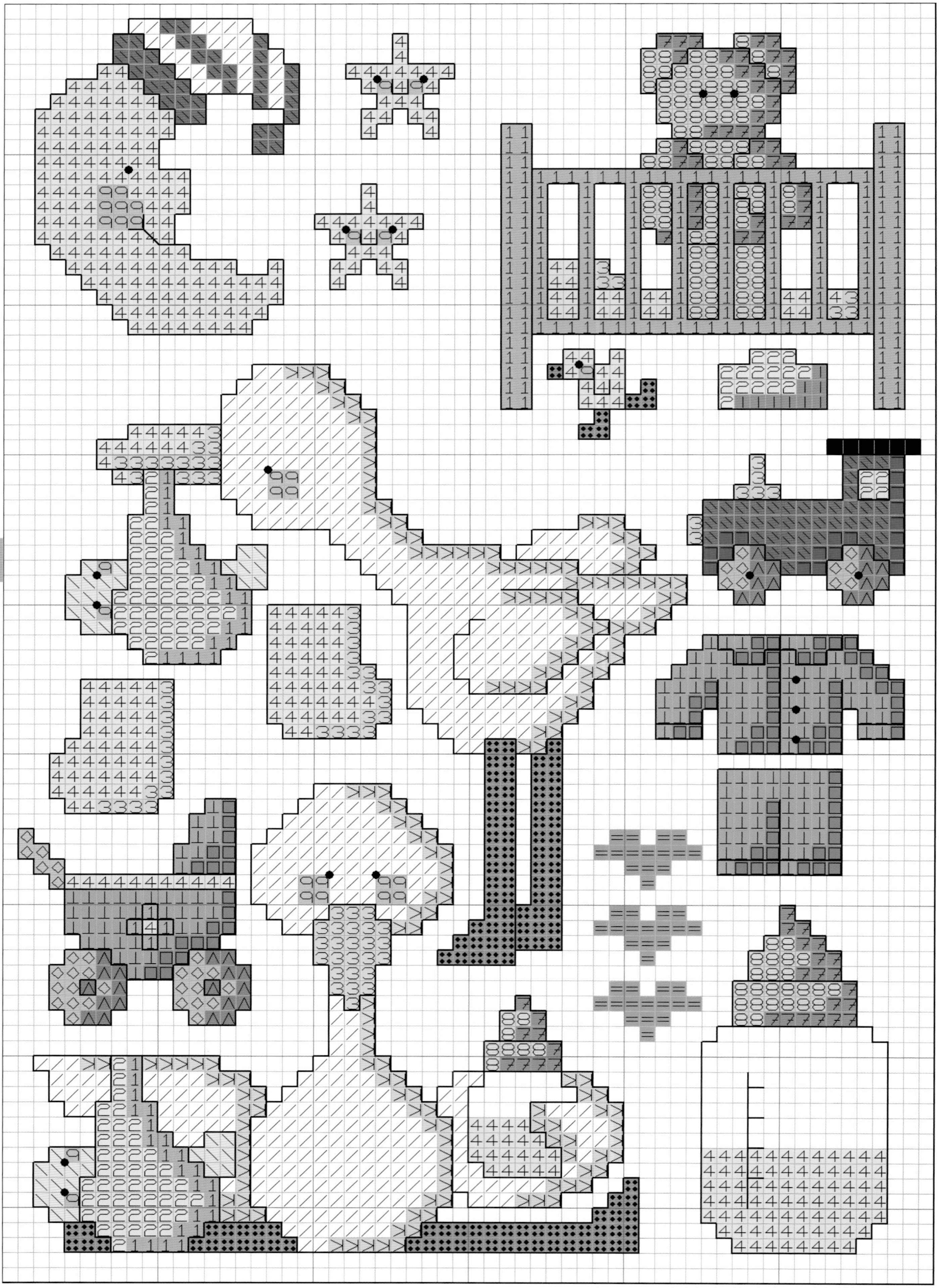

Birds

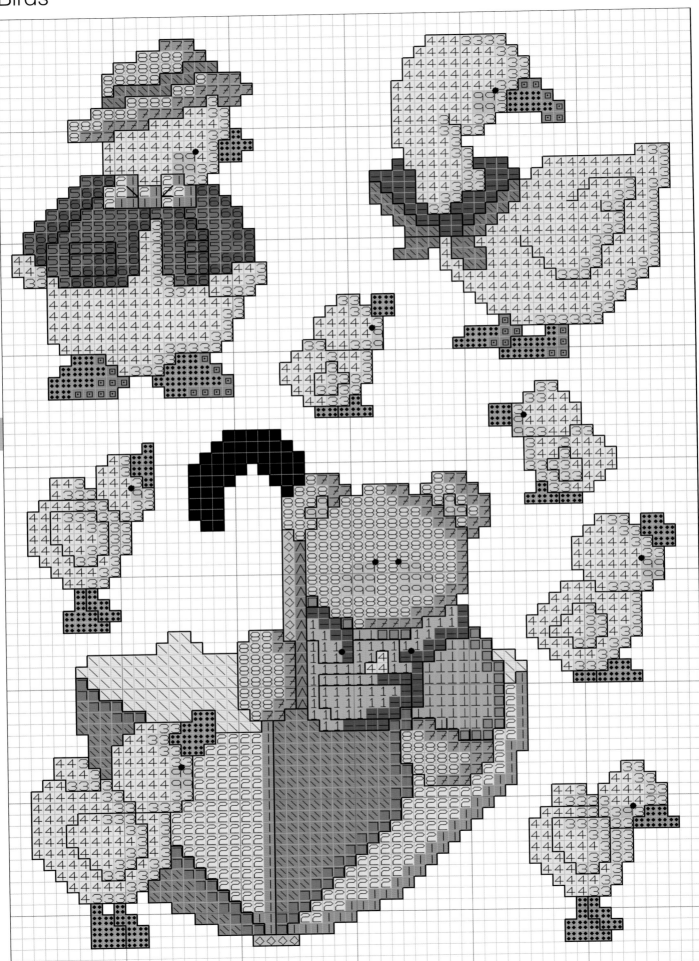

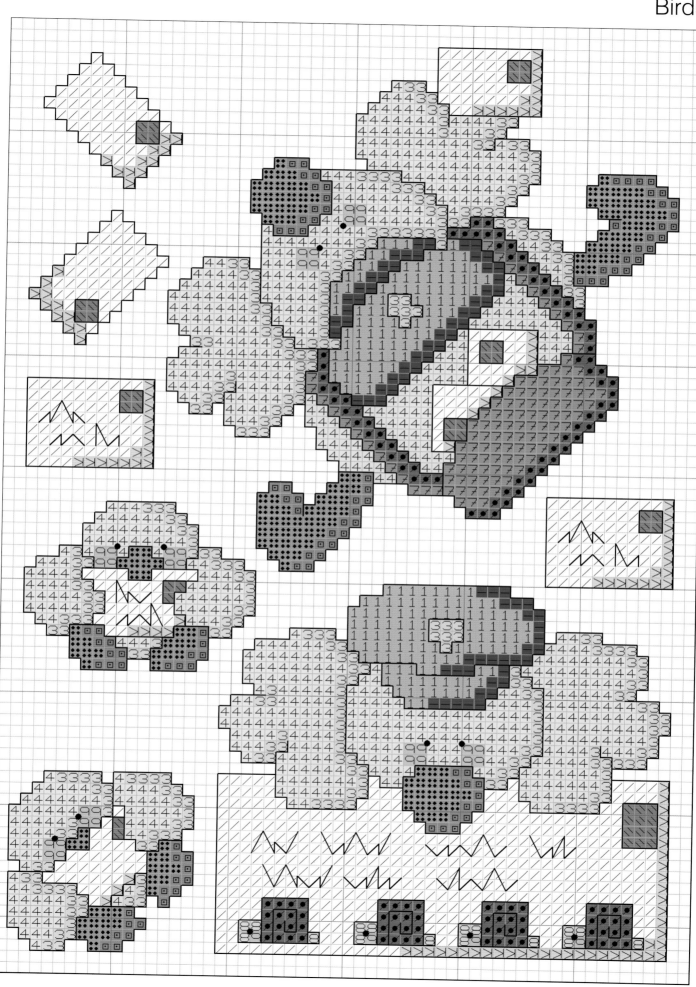

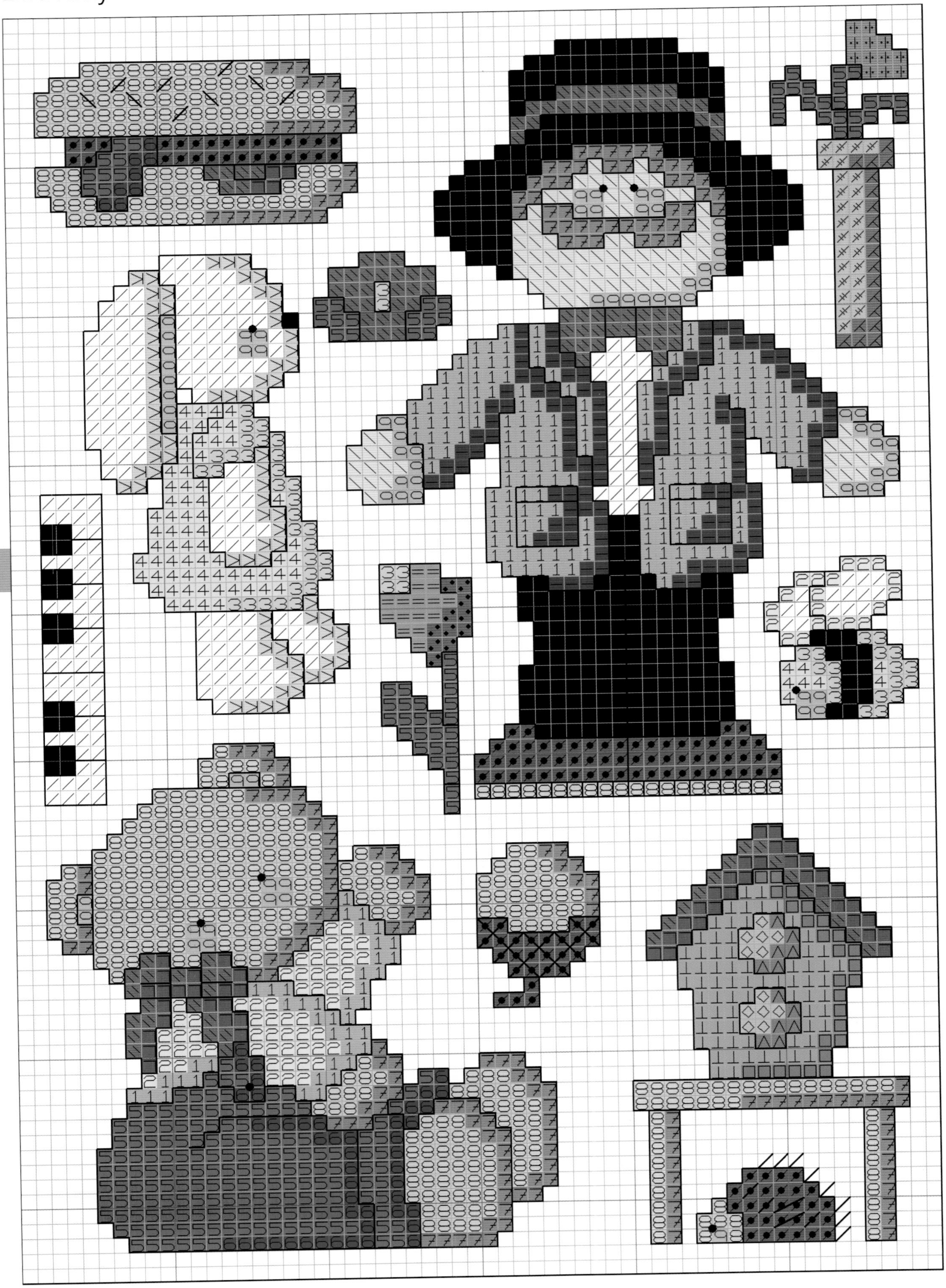

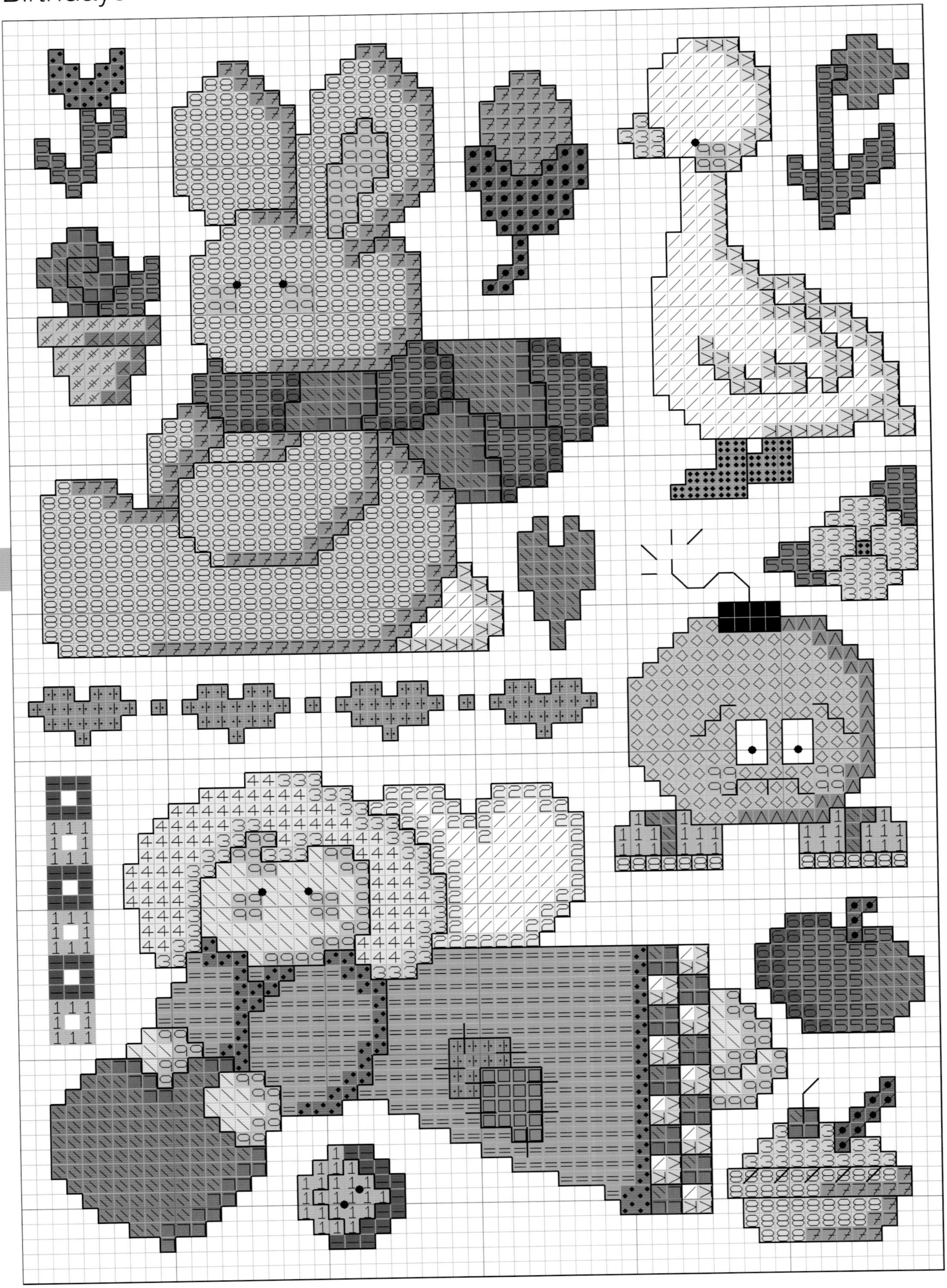

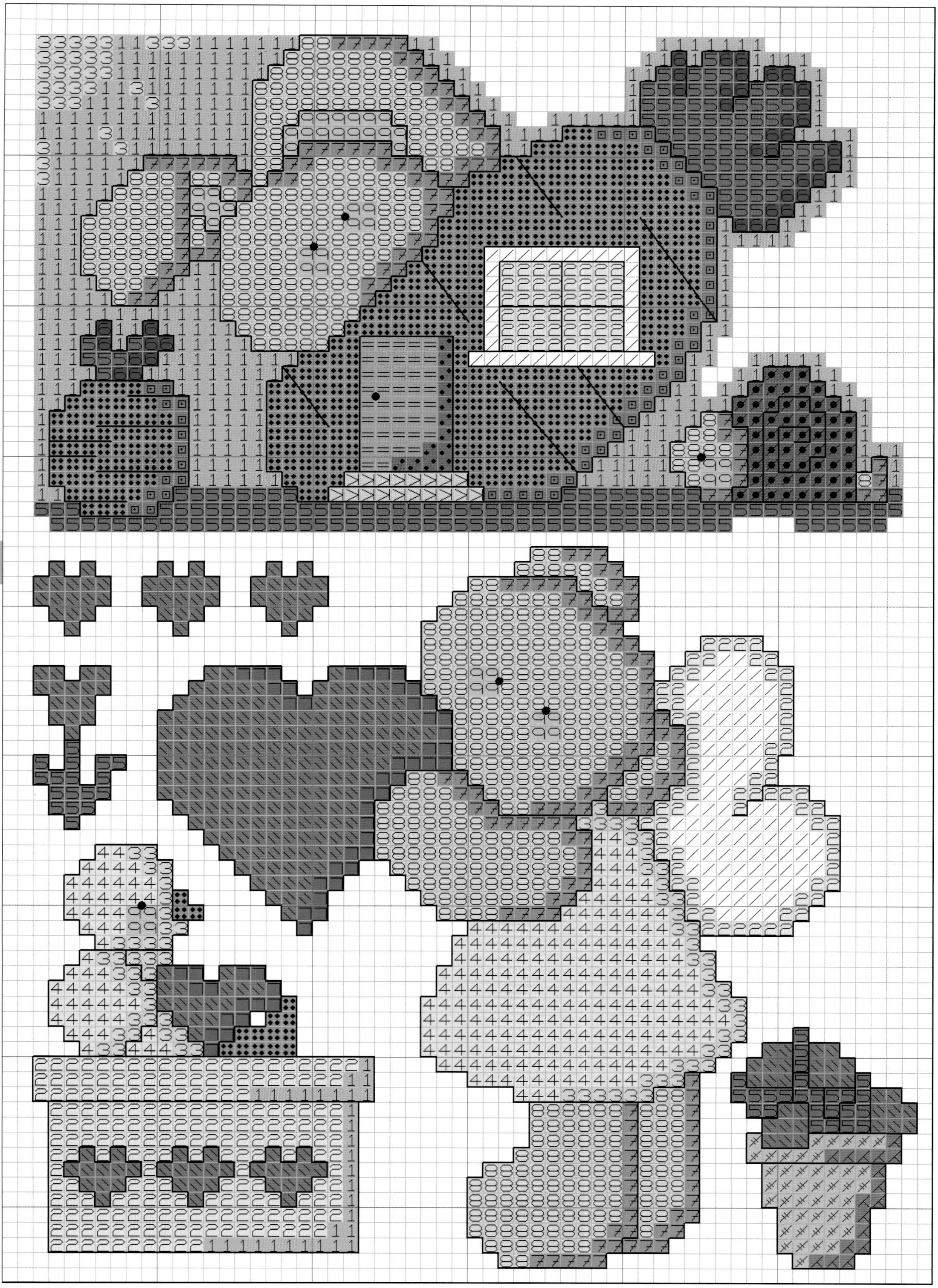

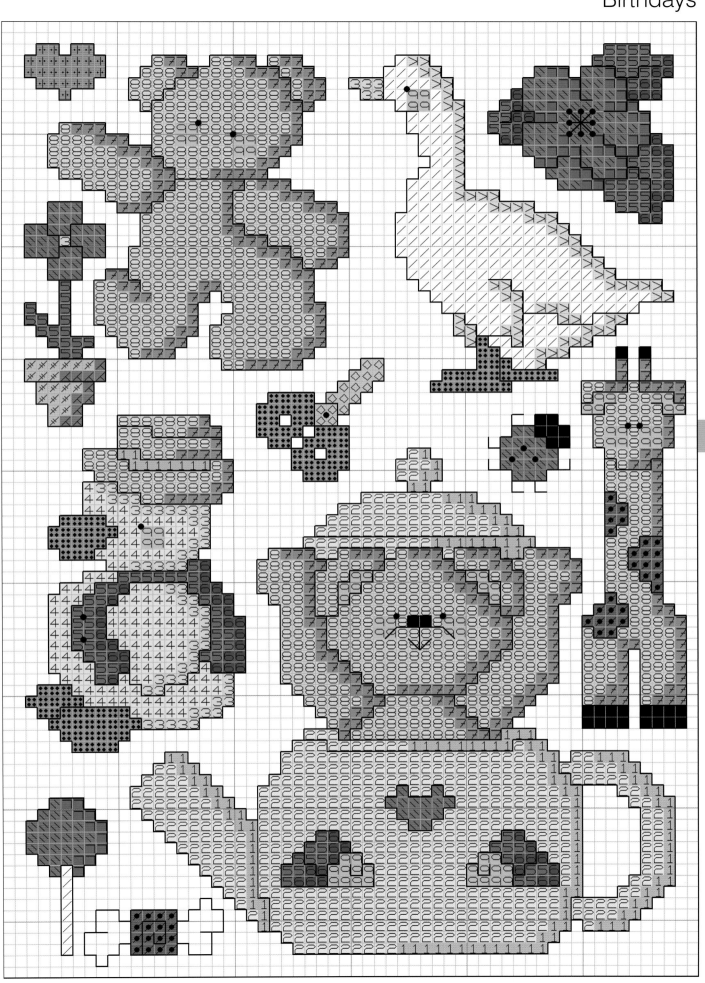

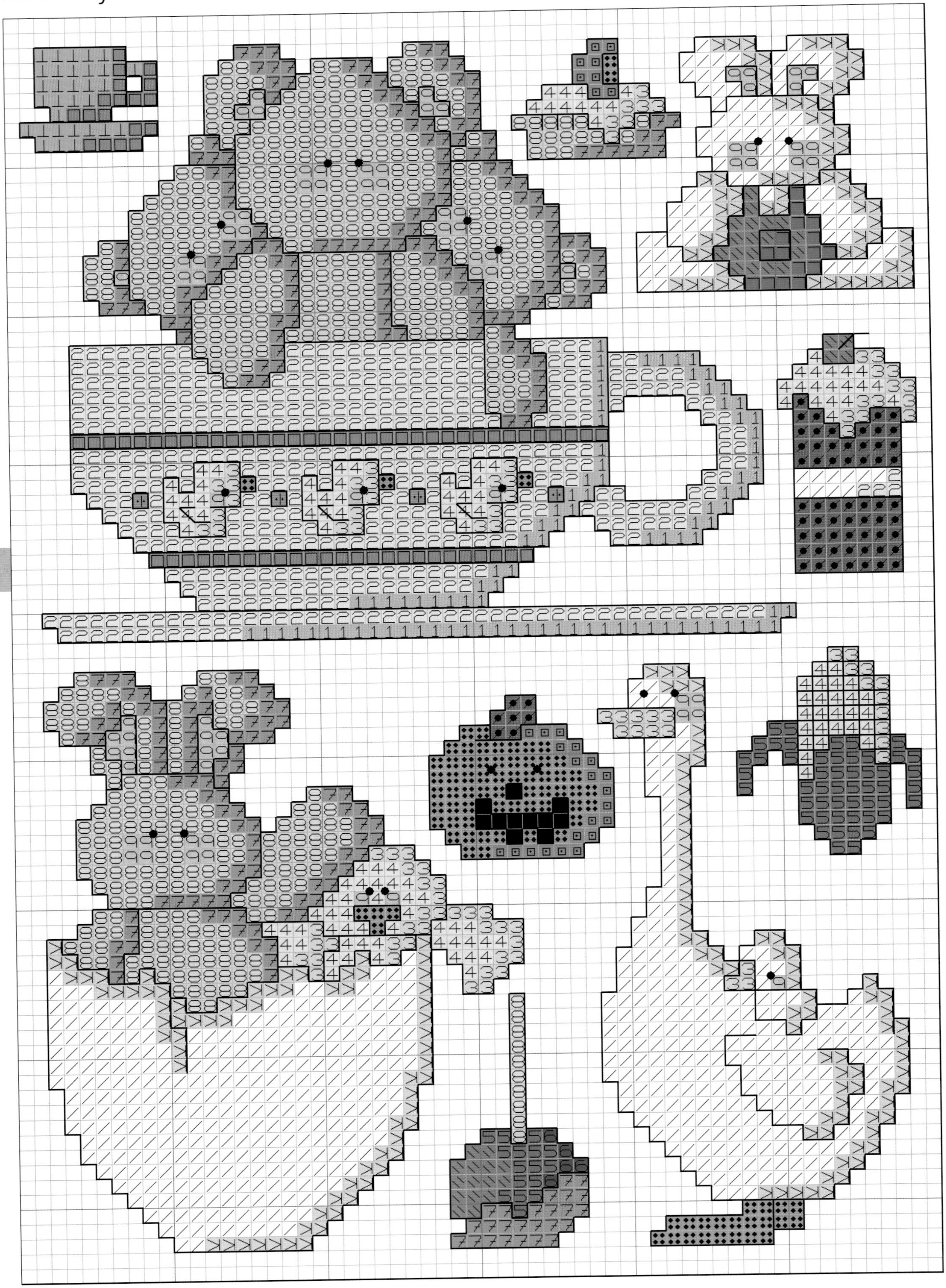

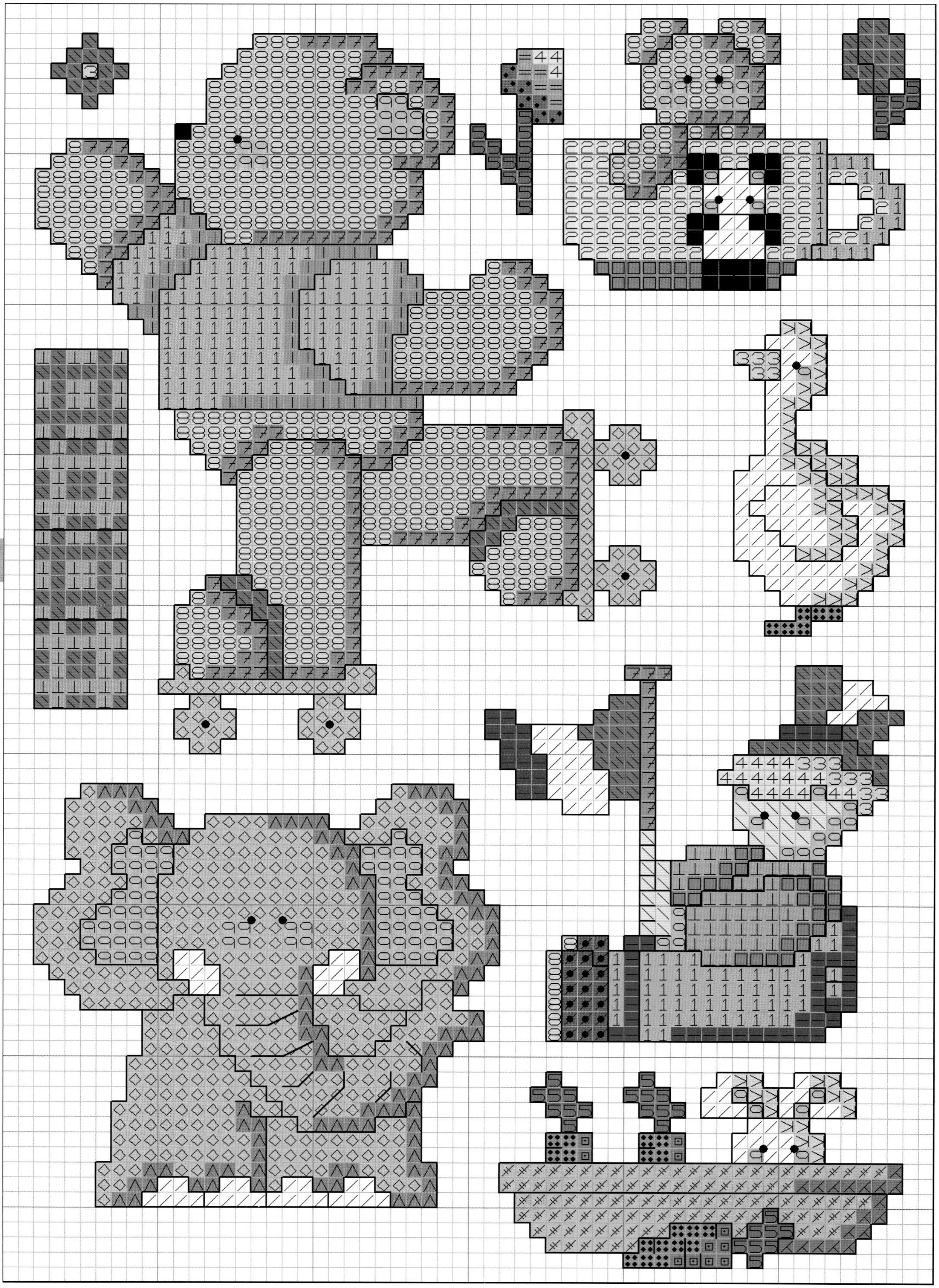

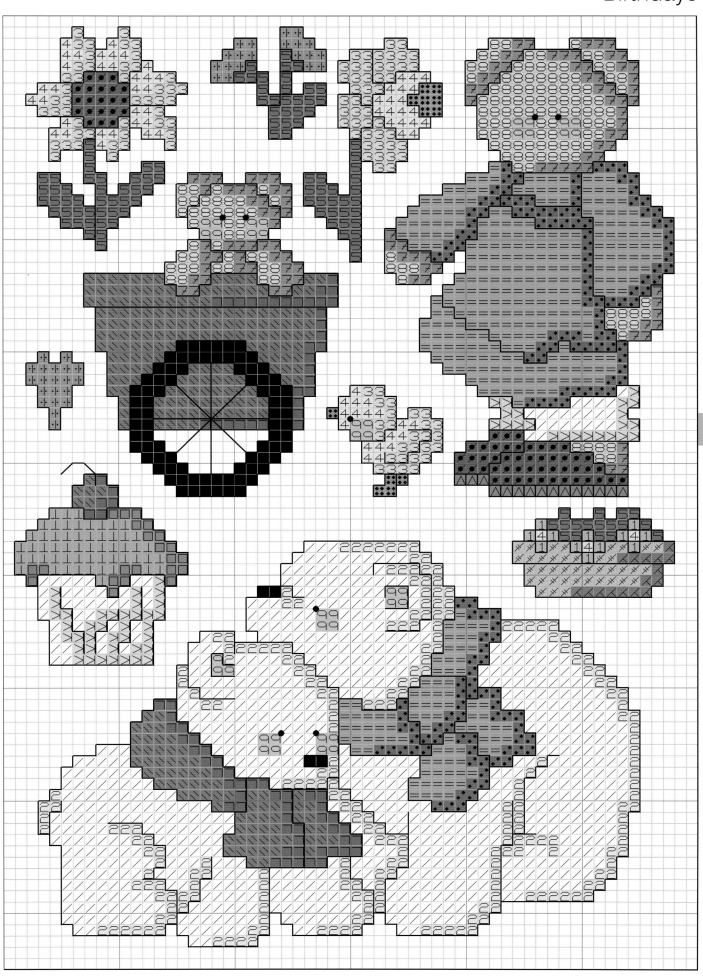

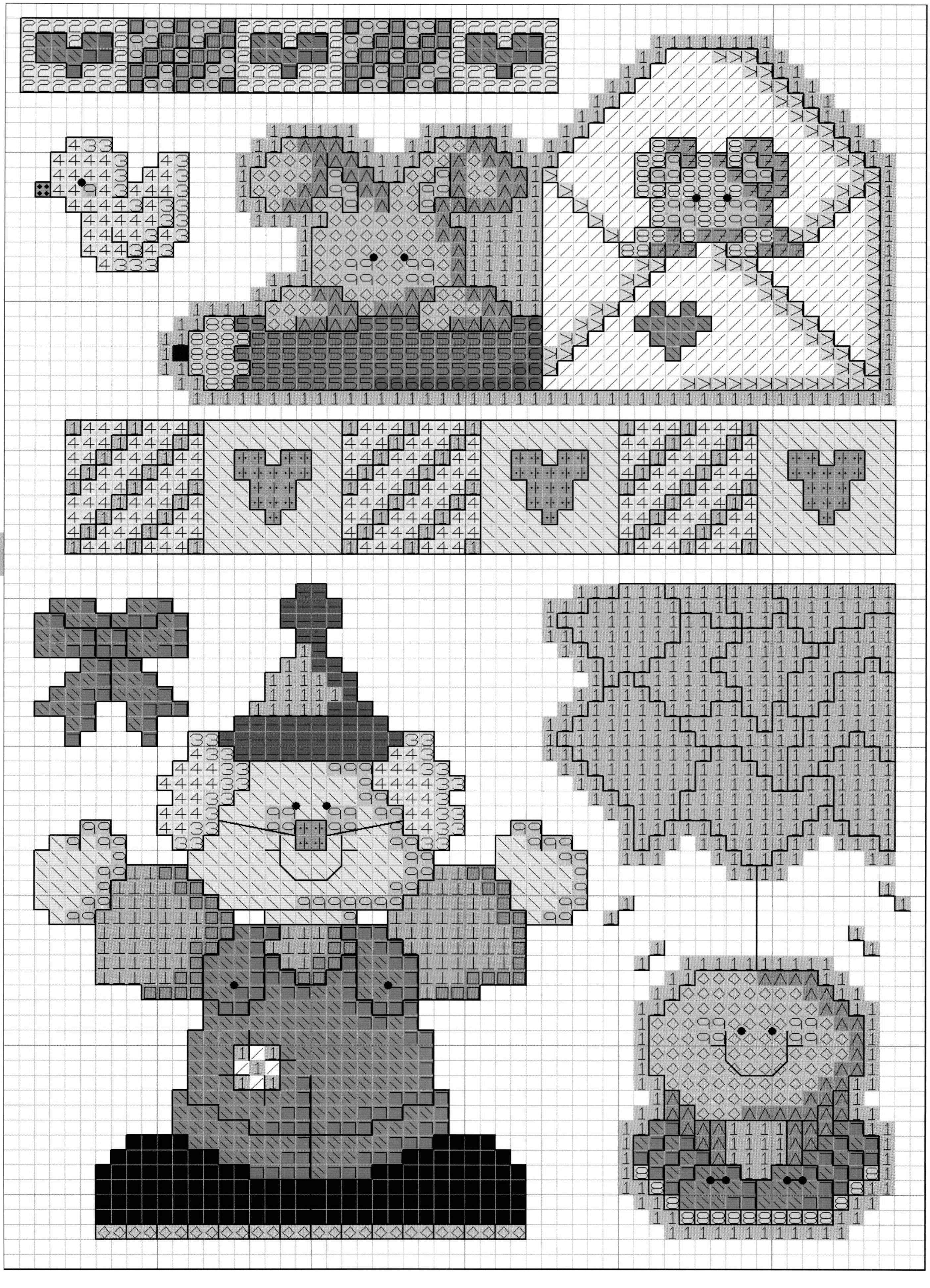

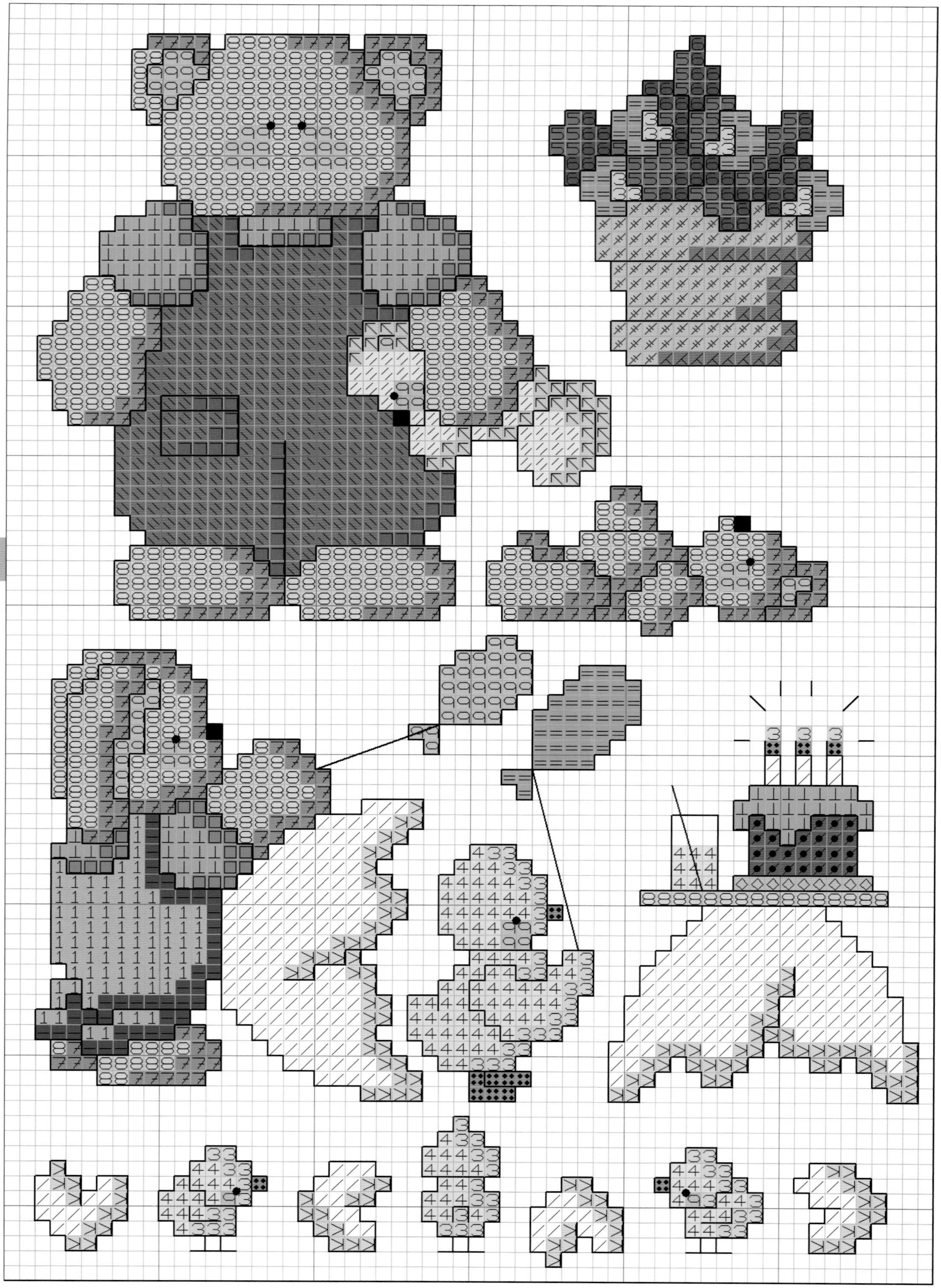

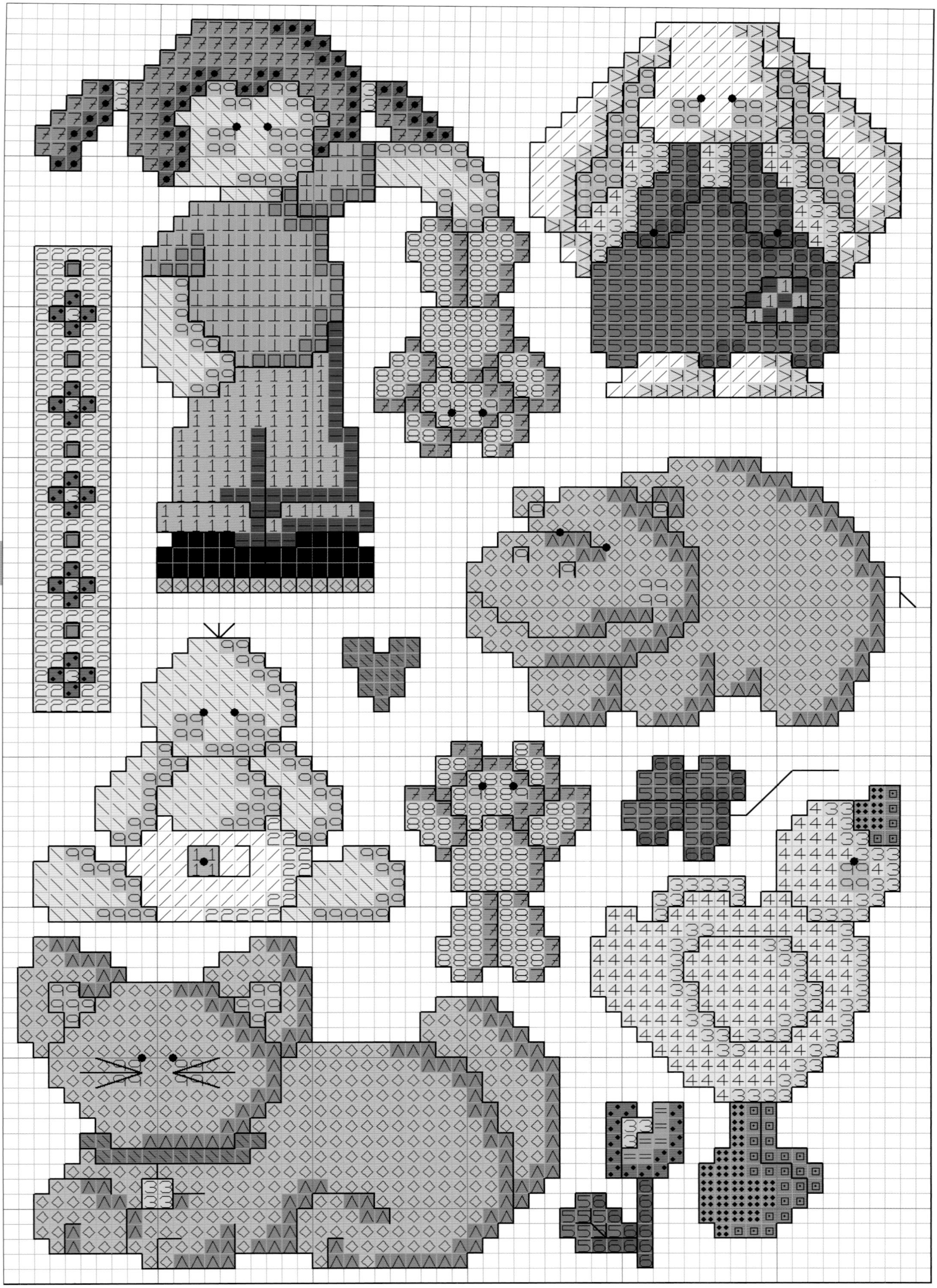

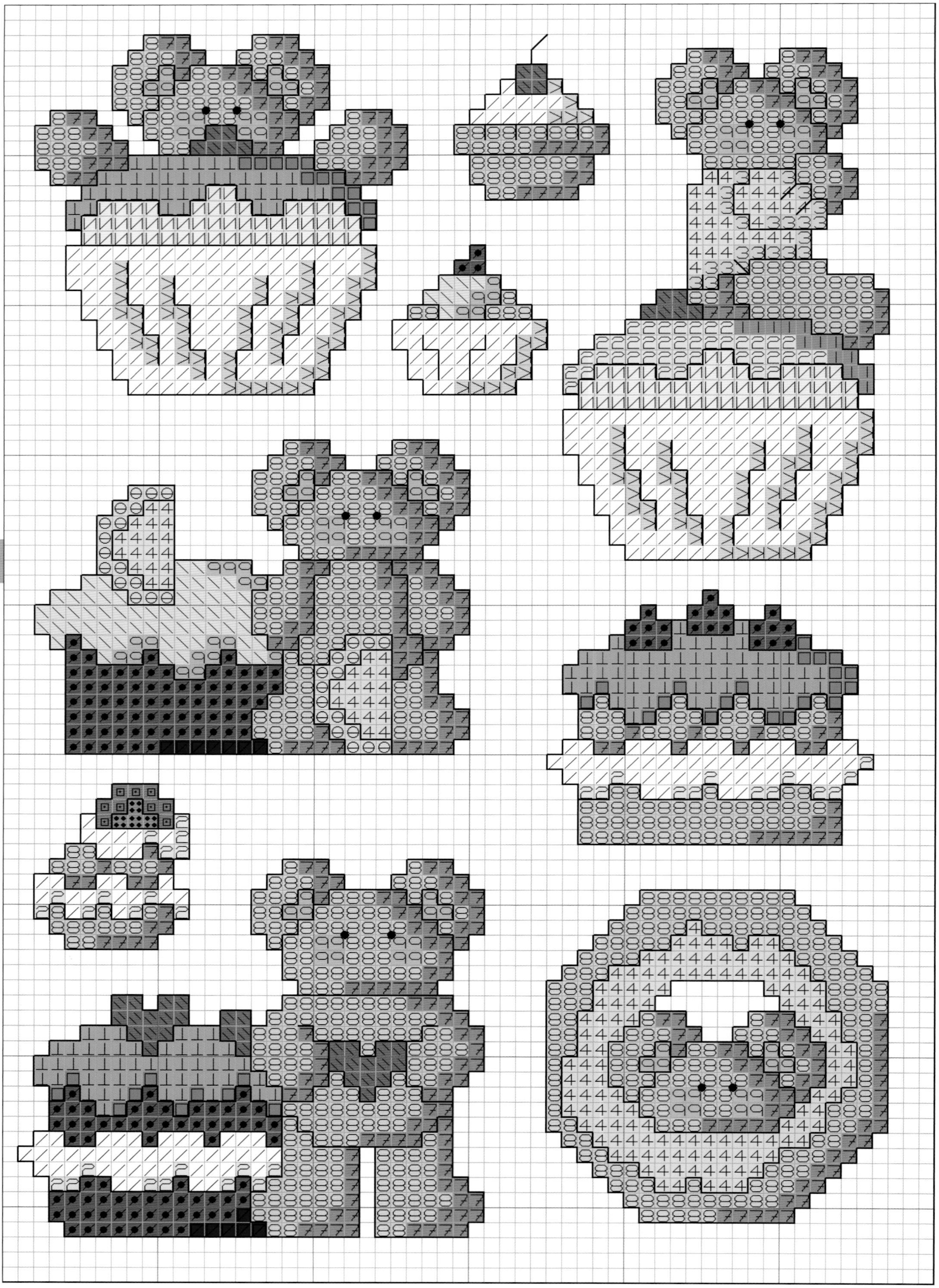

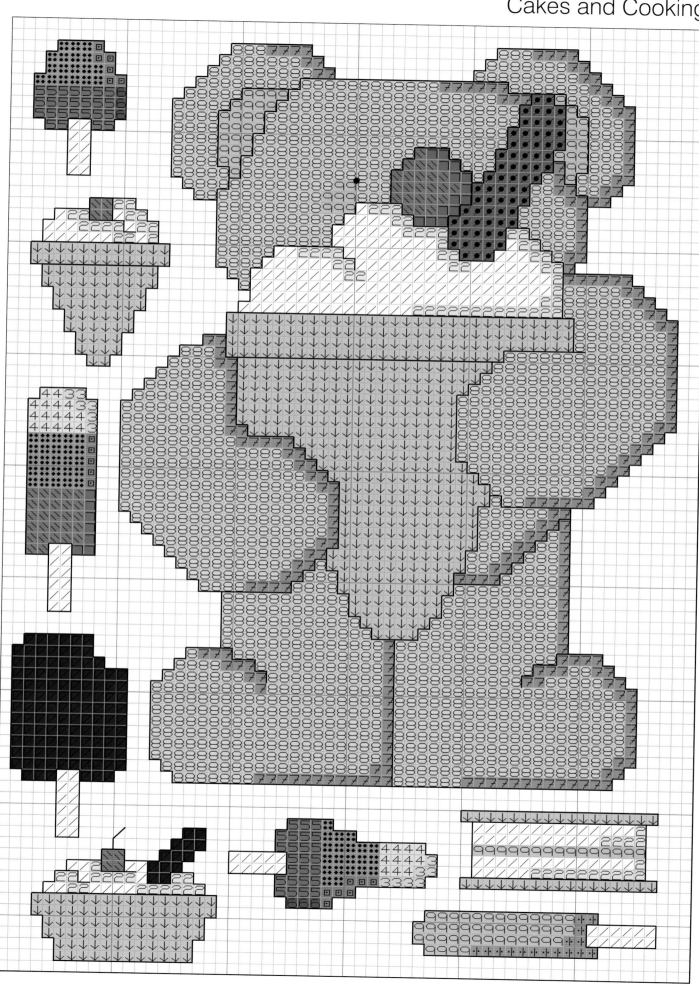

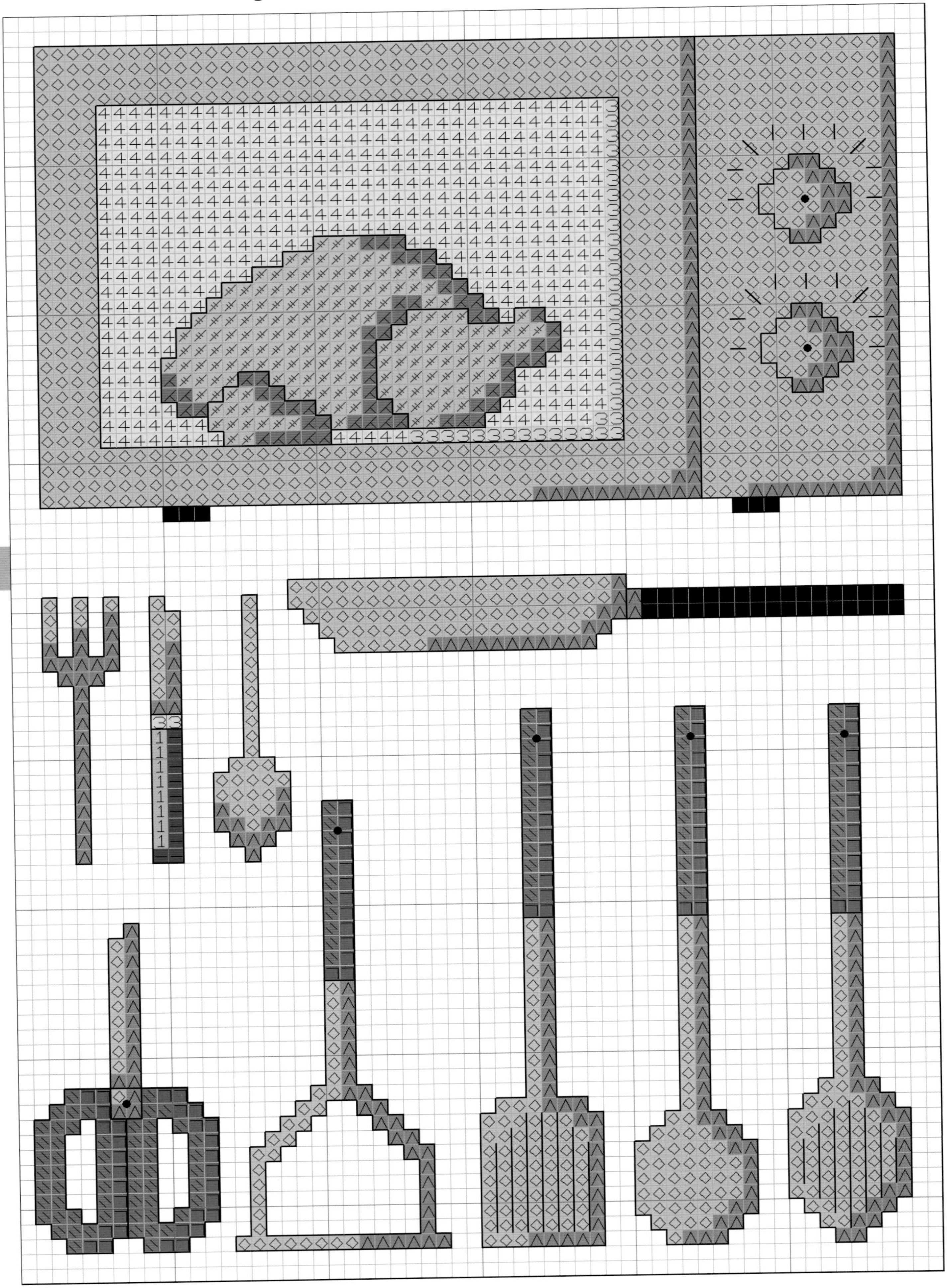

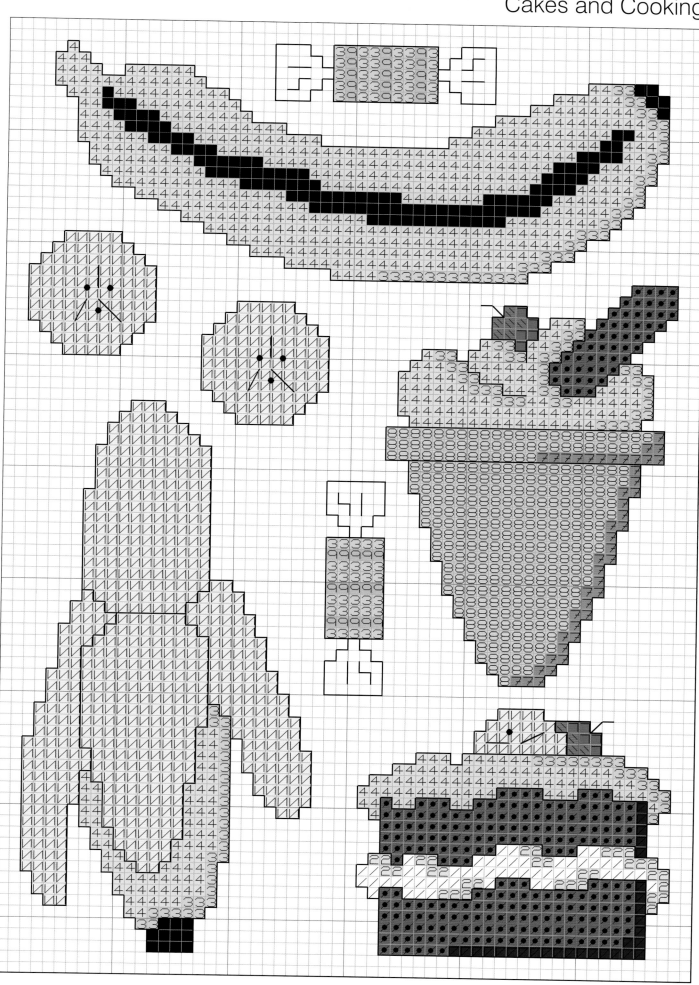

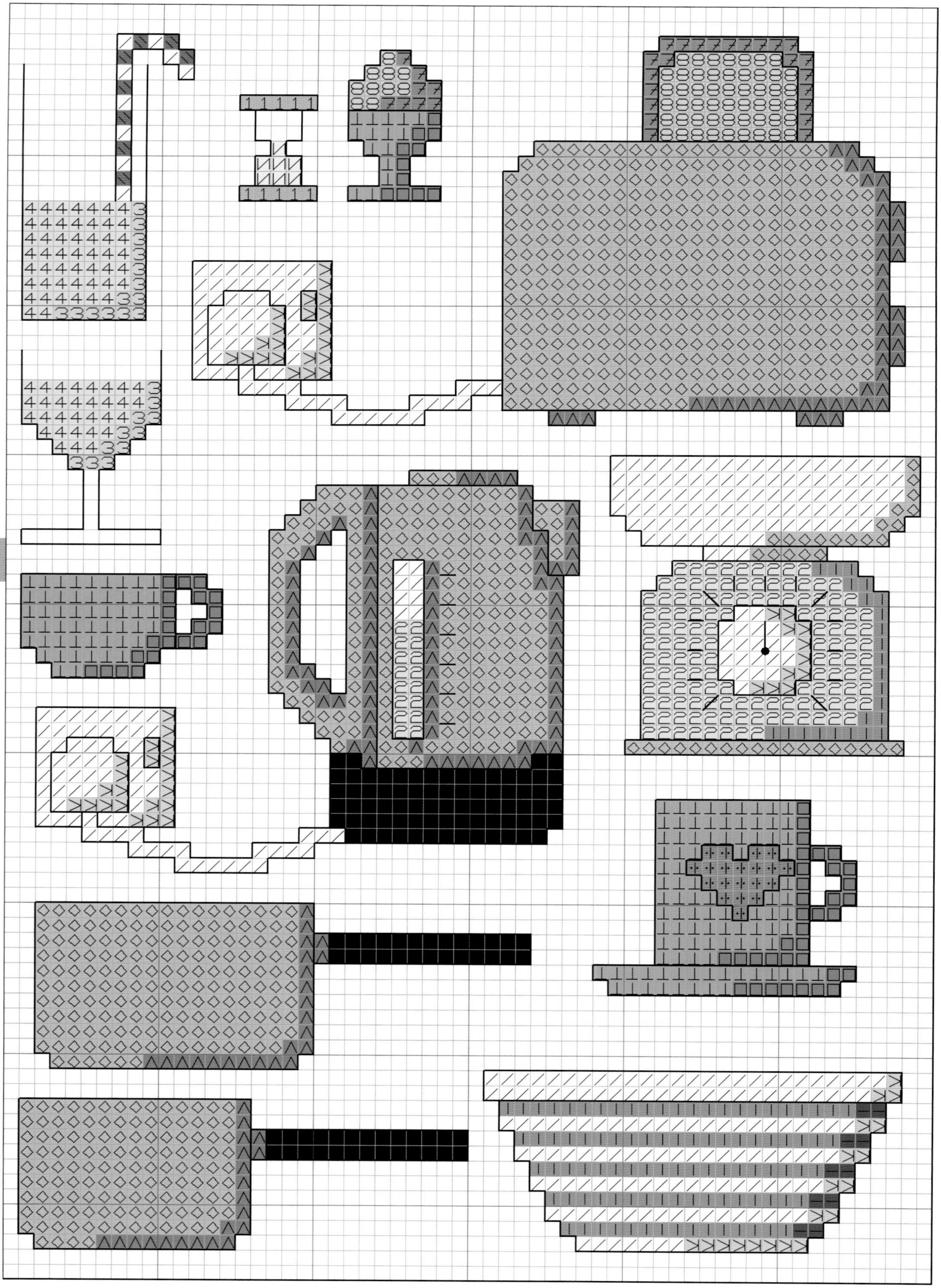

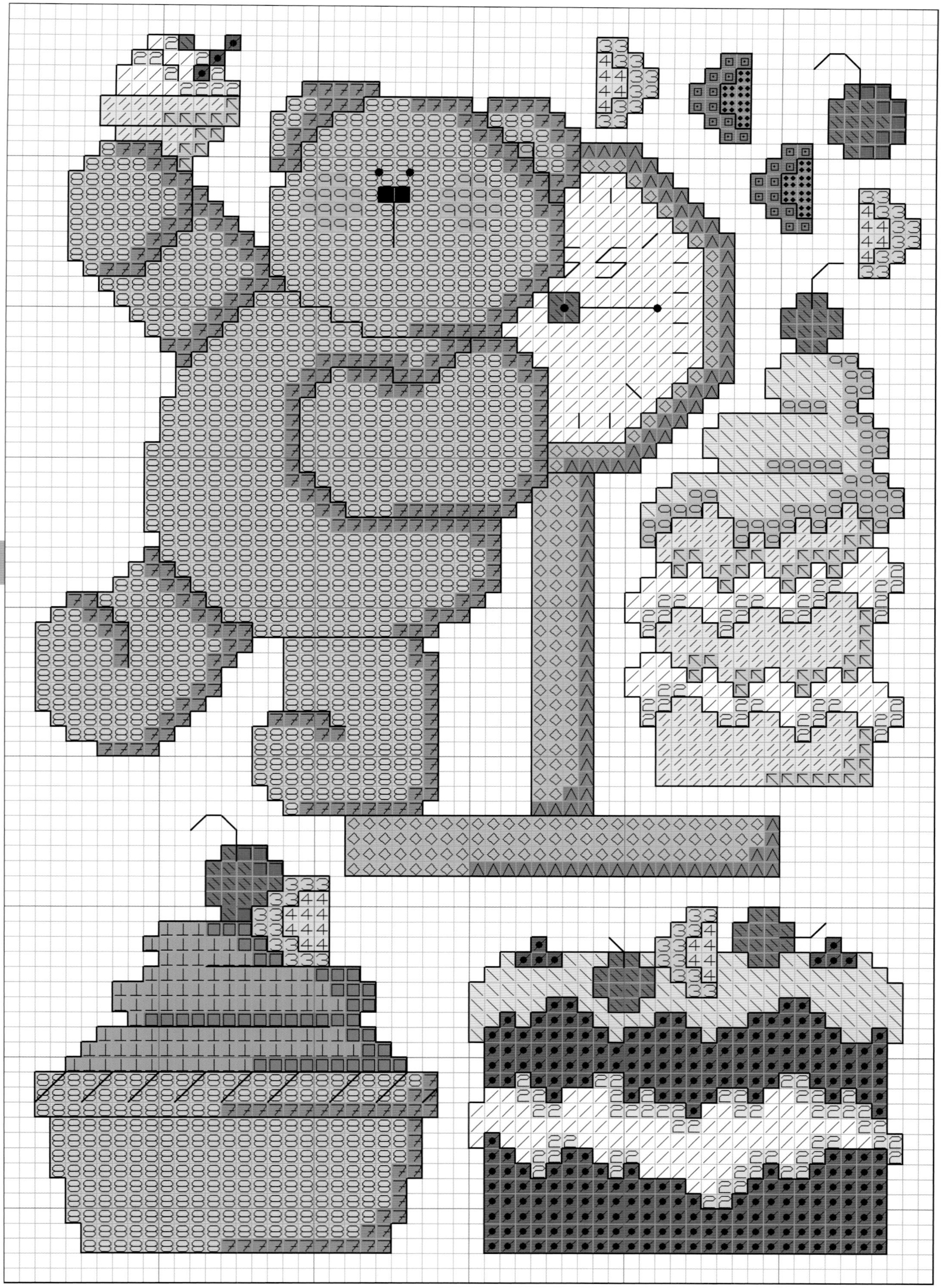

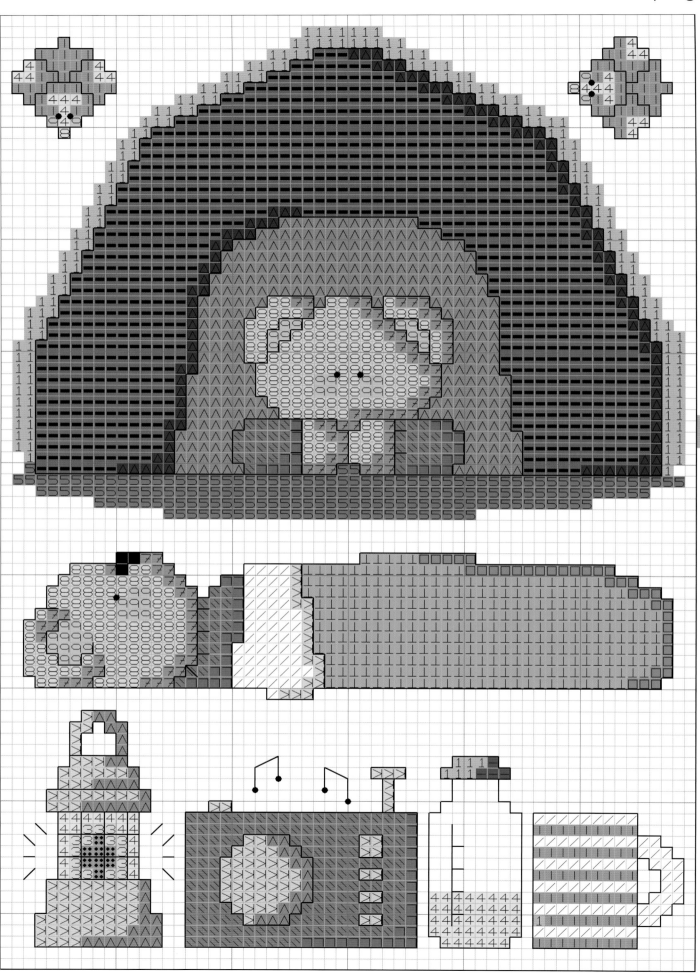

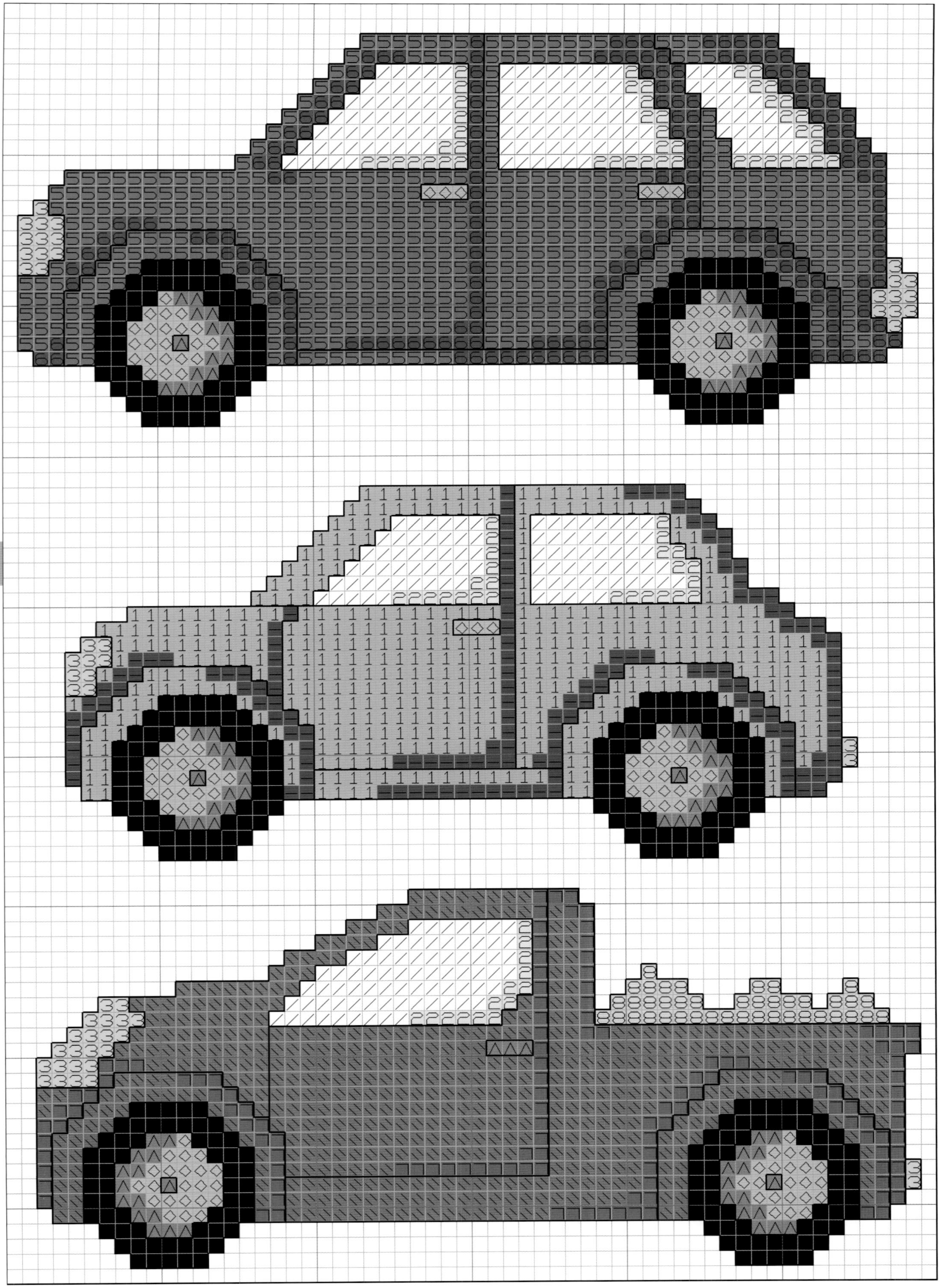

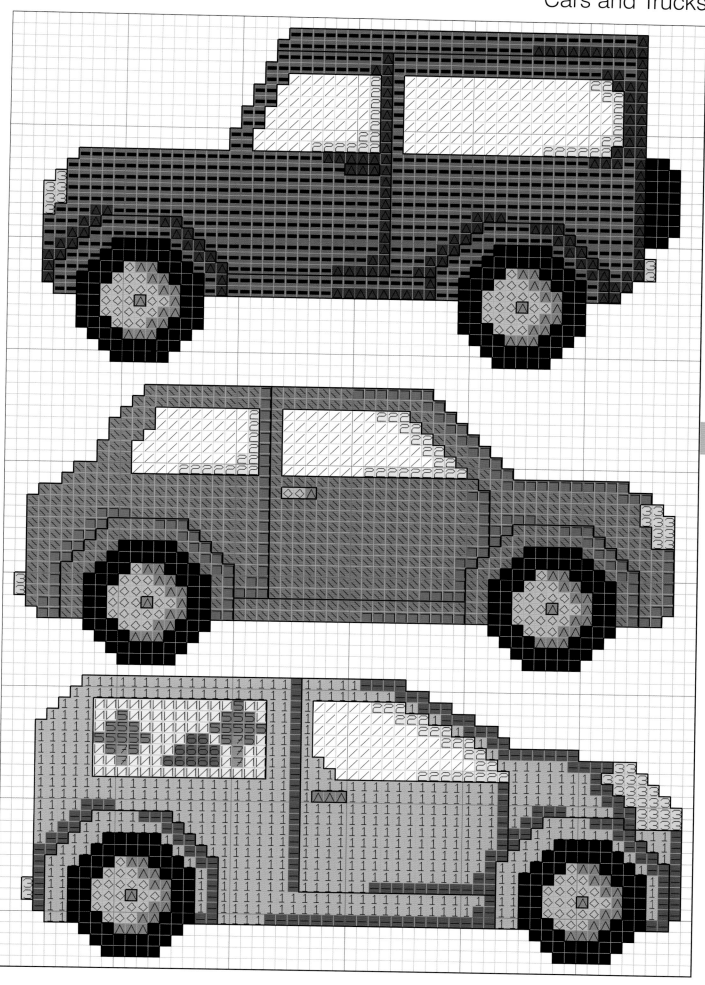

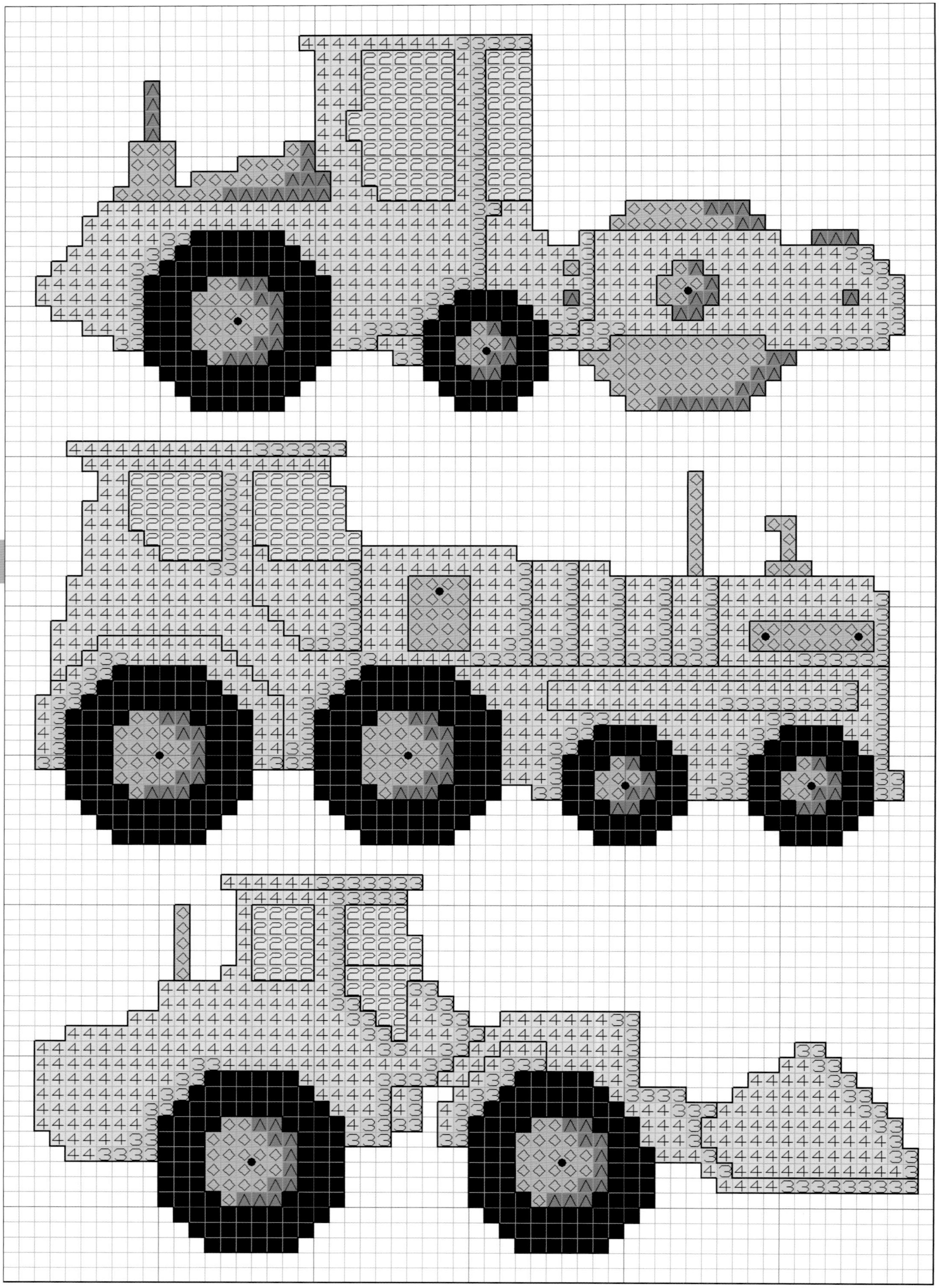

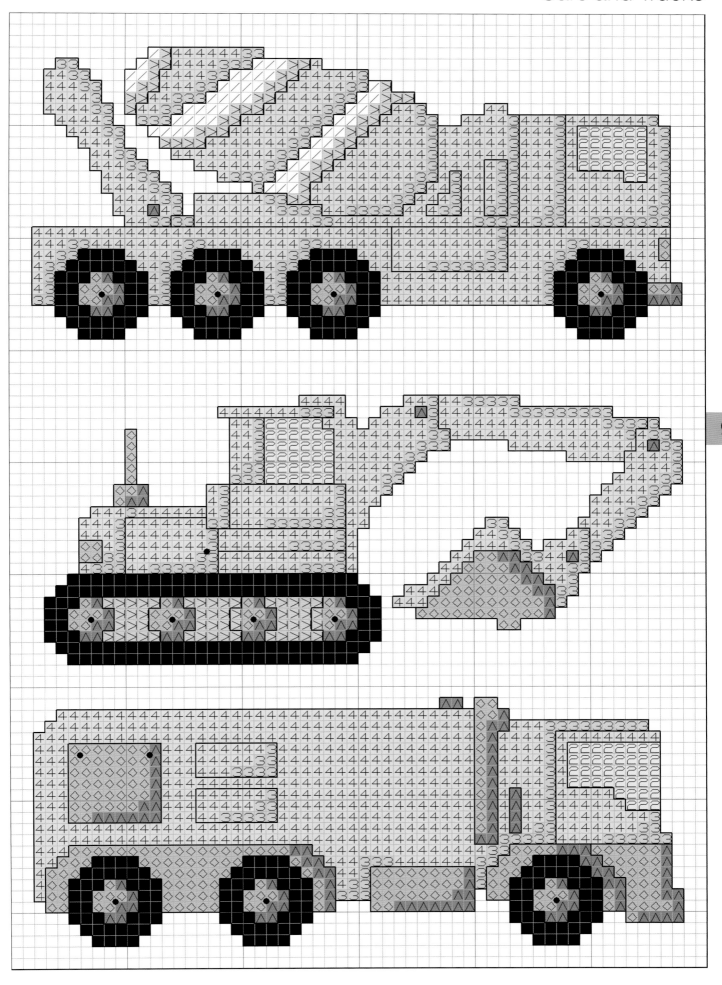

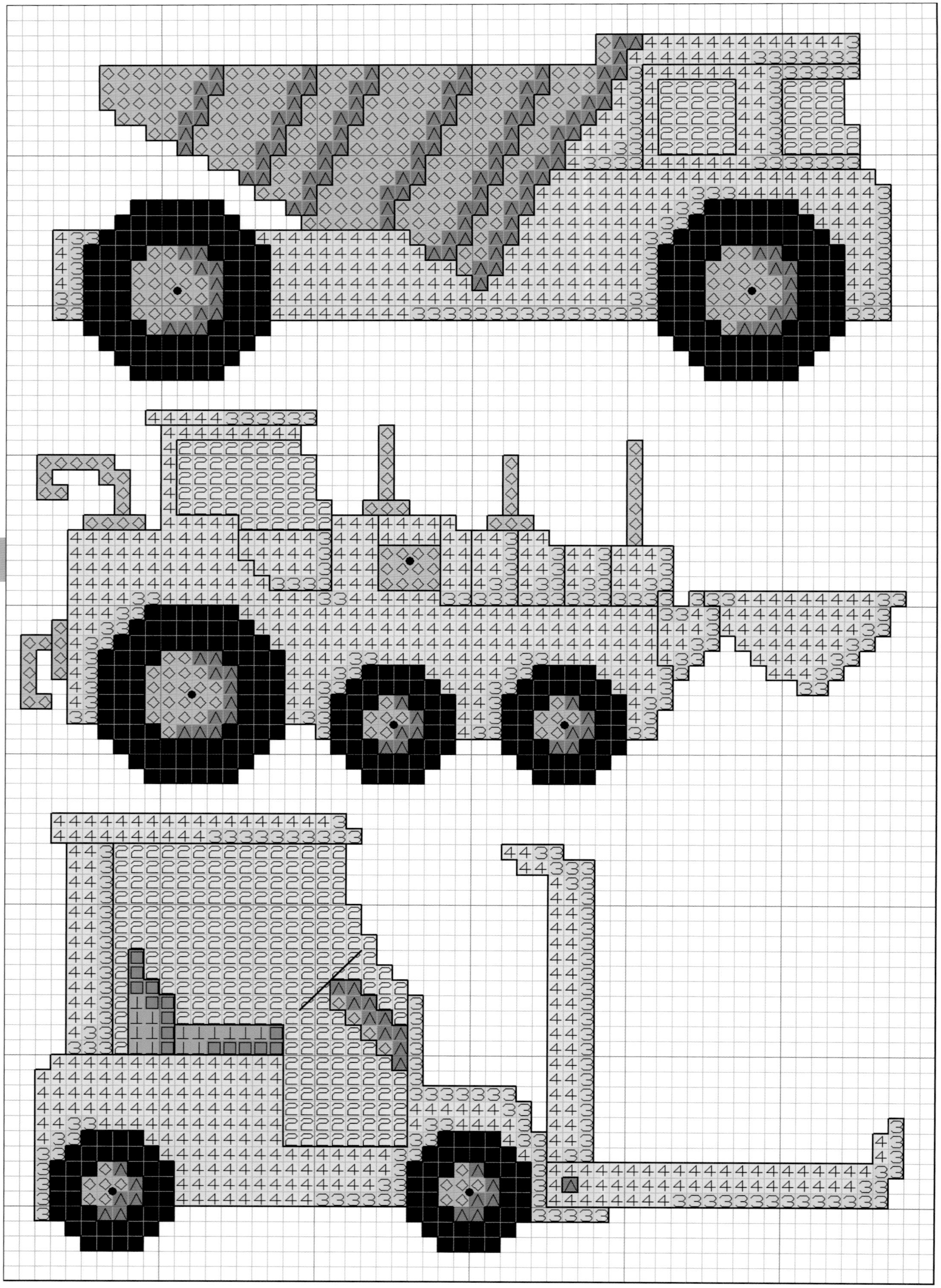

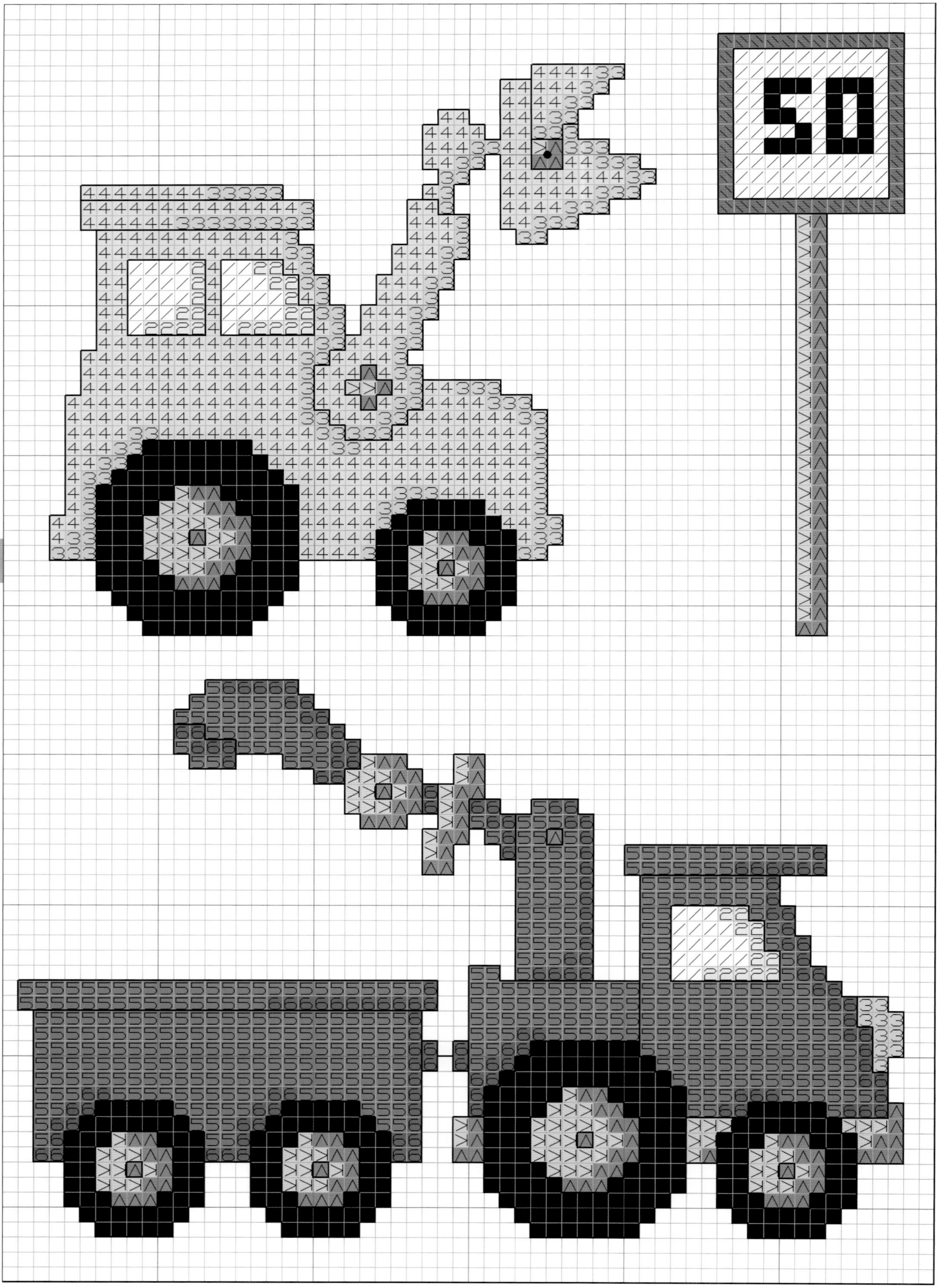

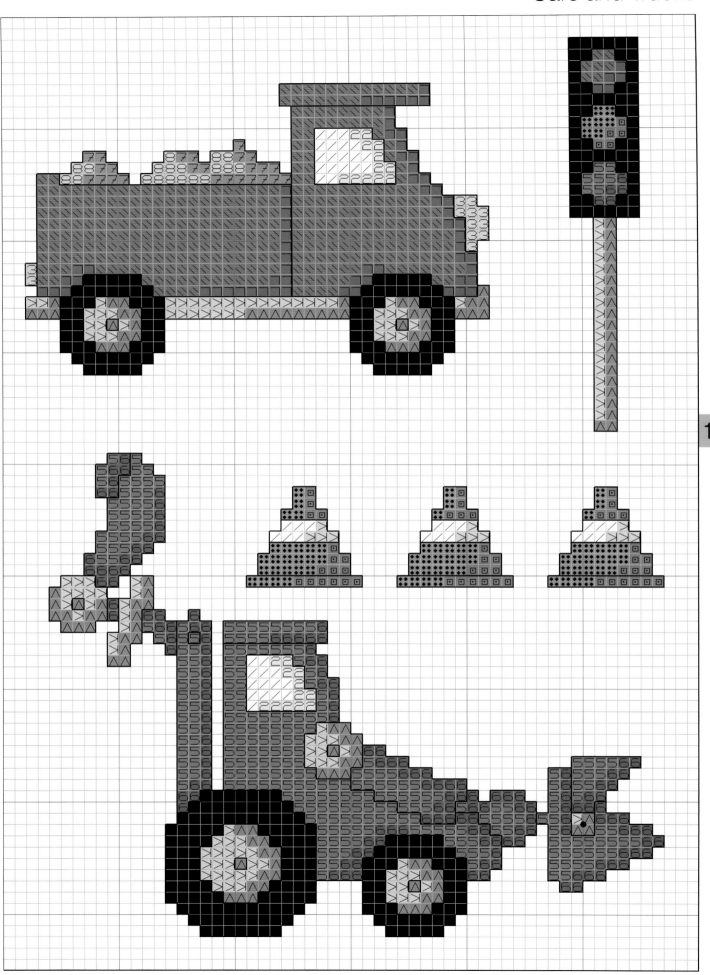

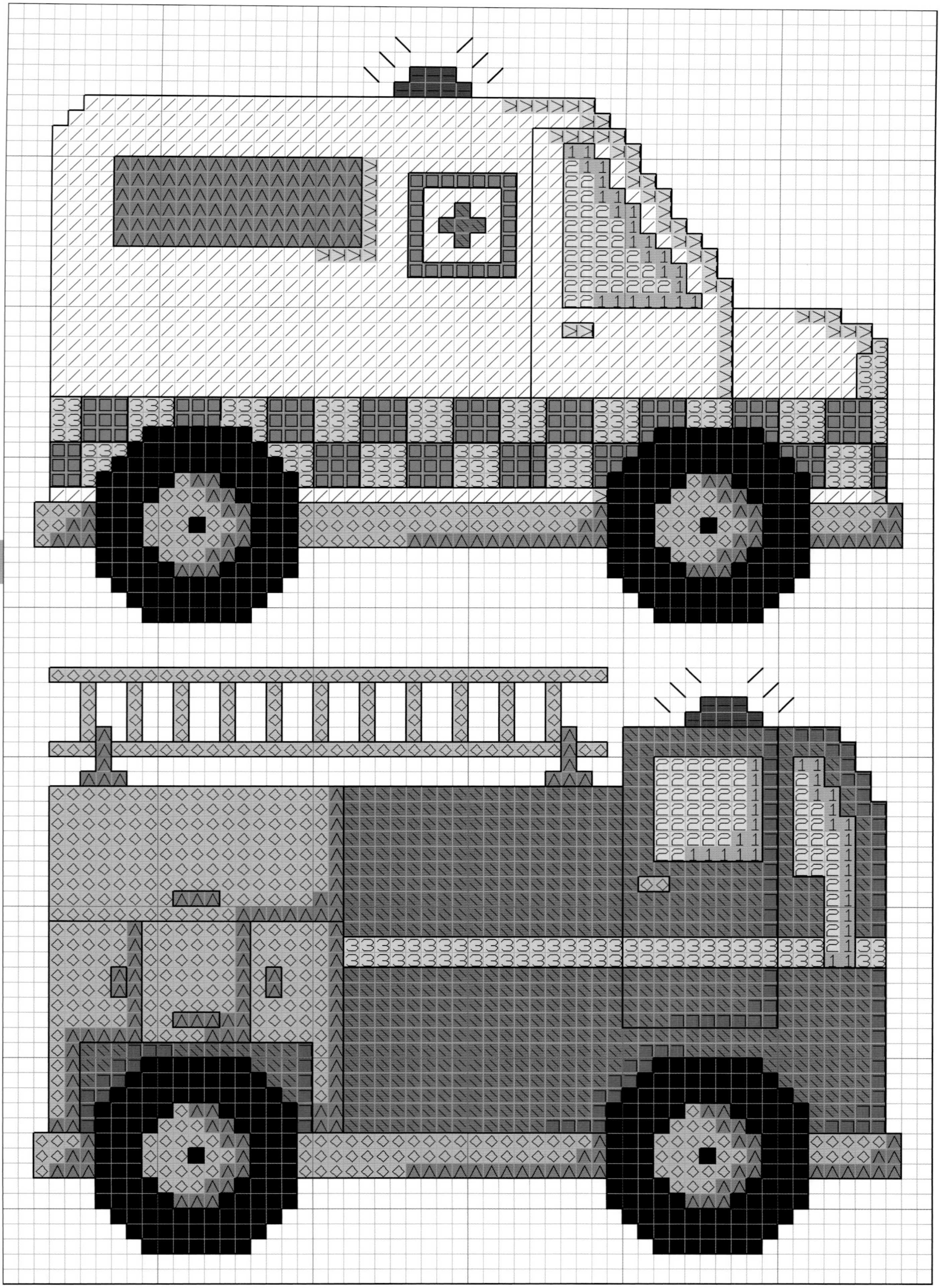

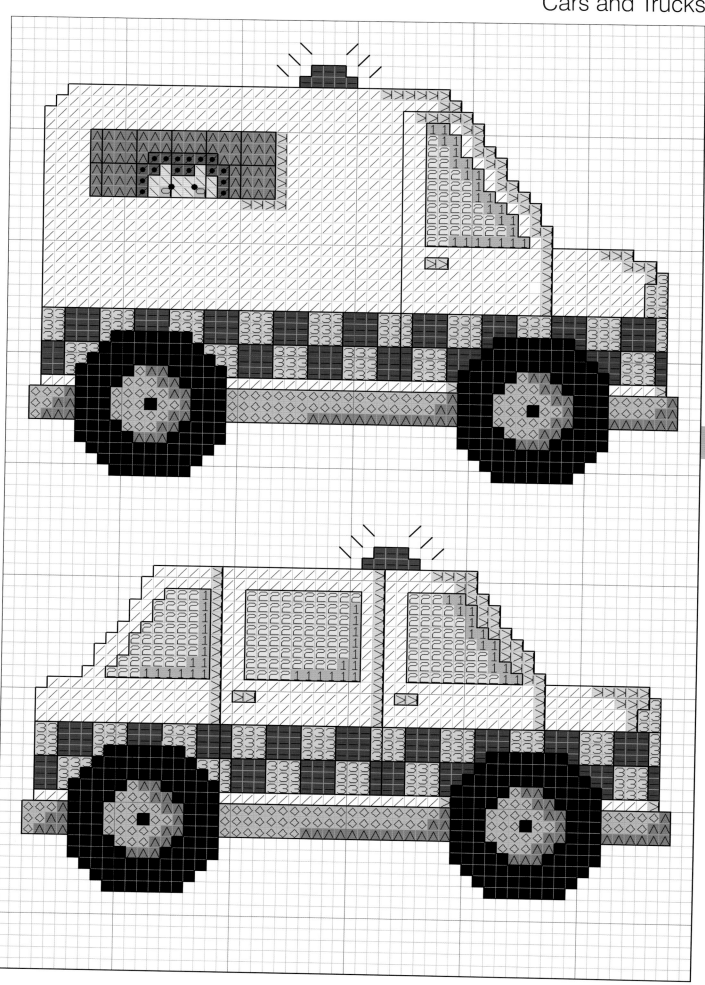

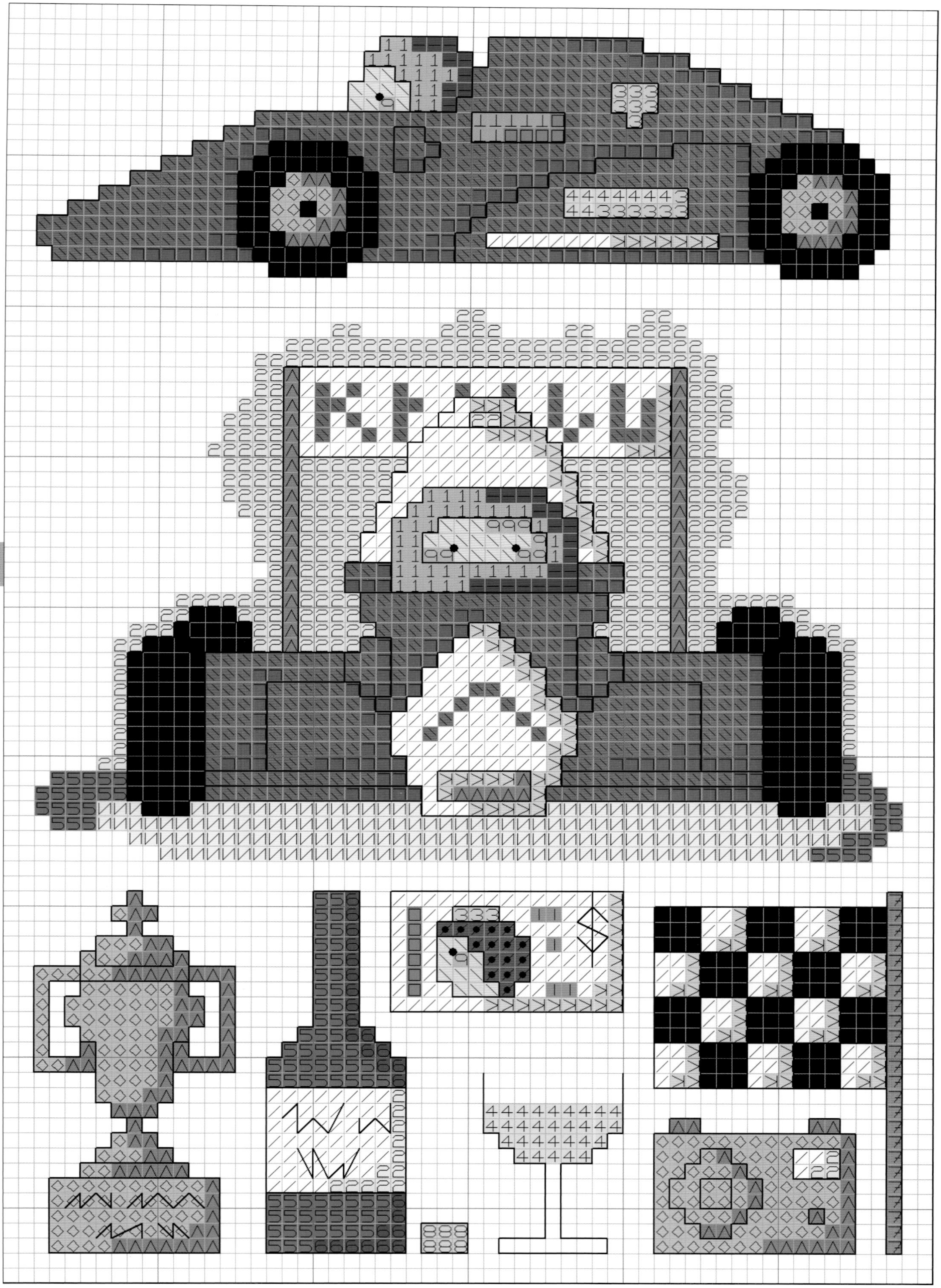

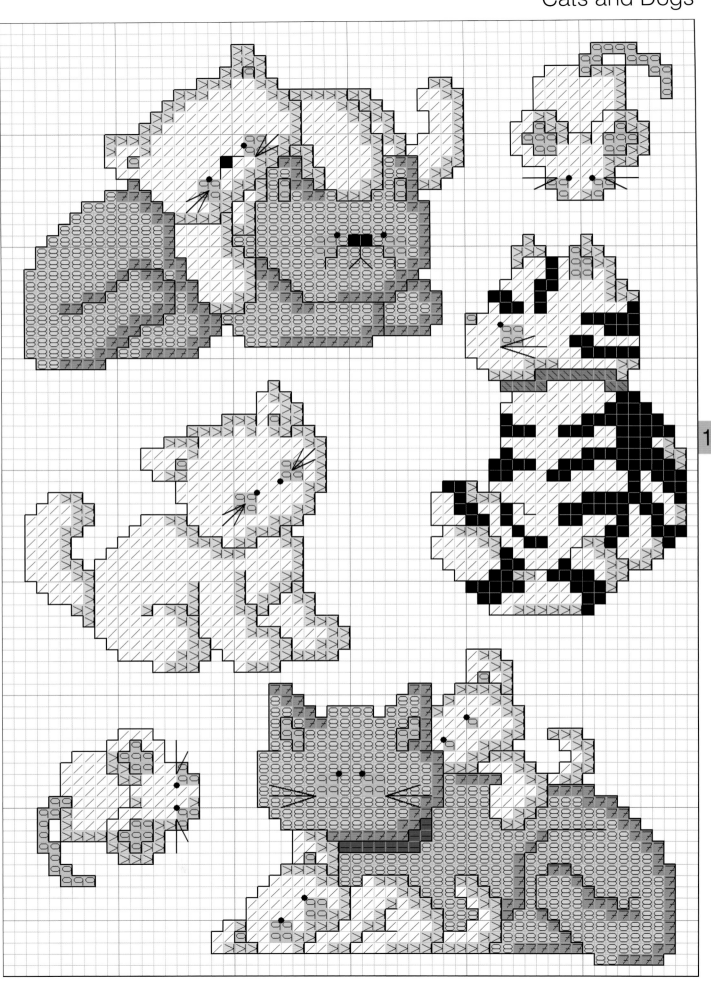

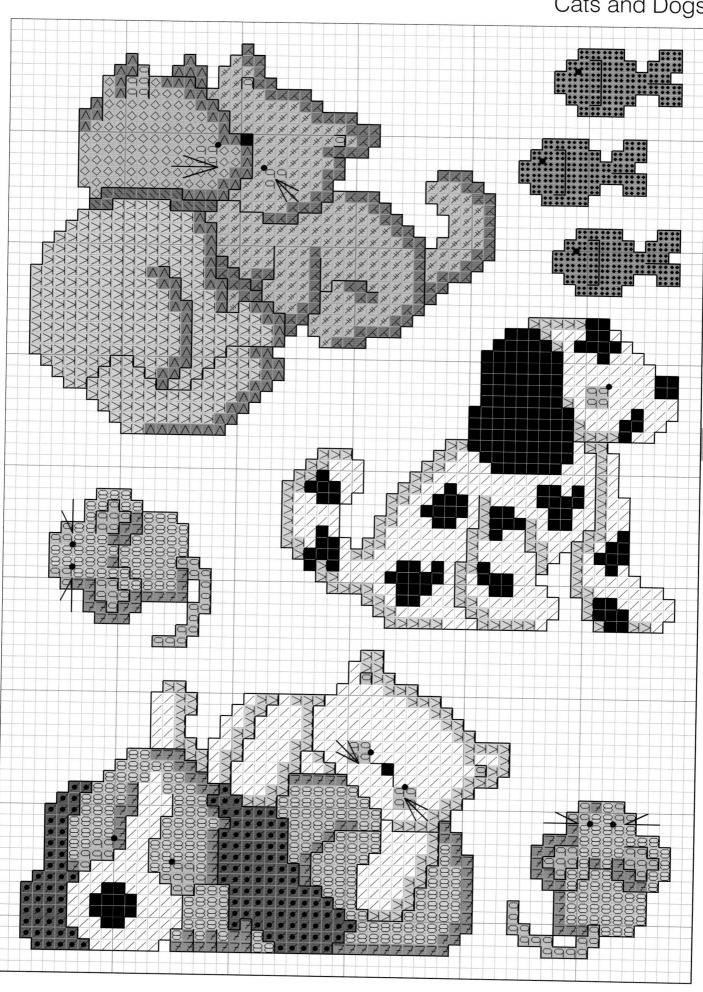

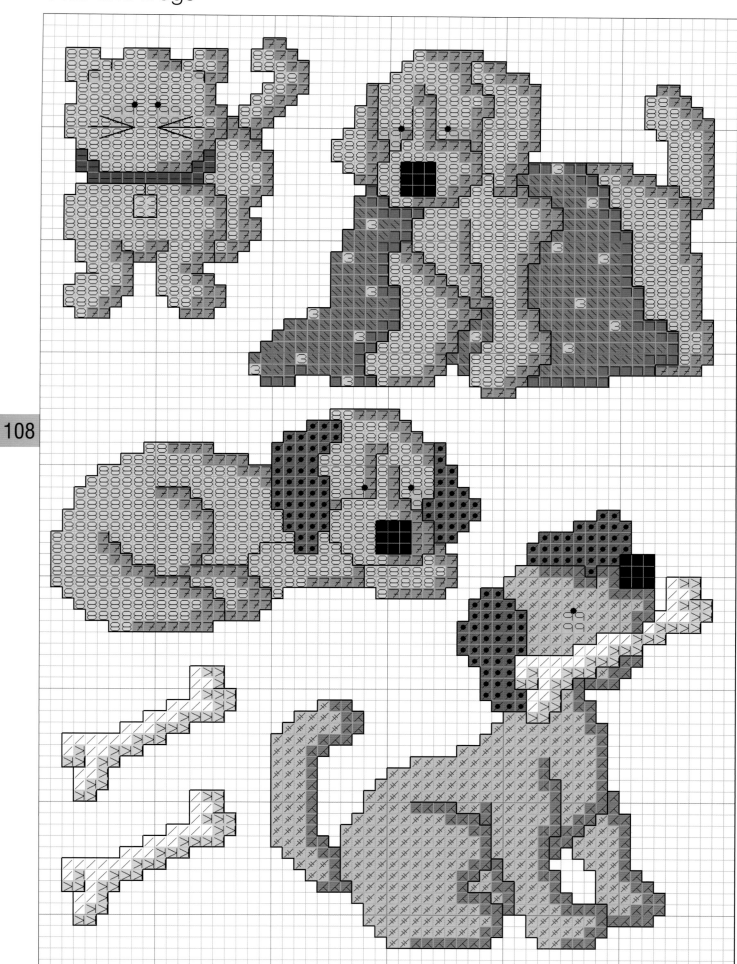

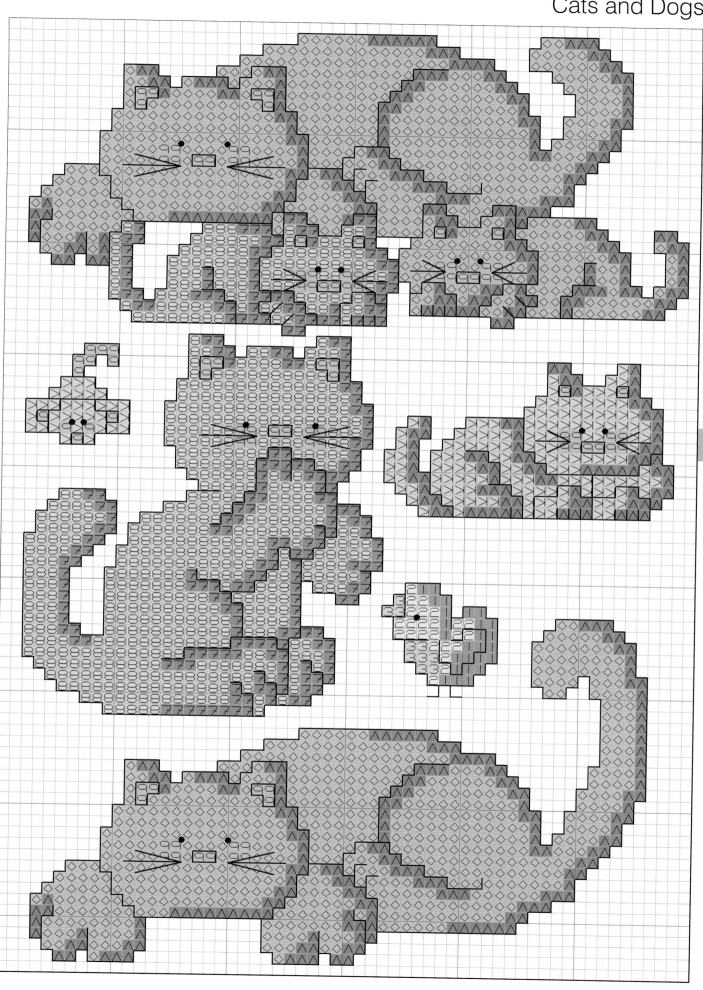

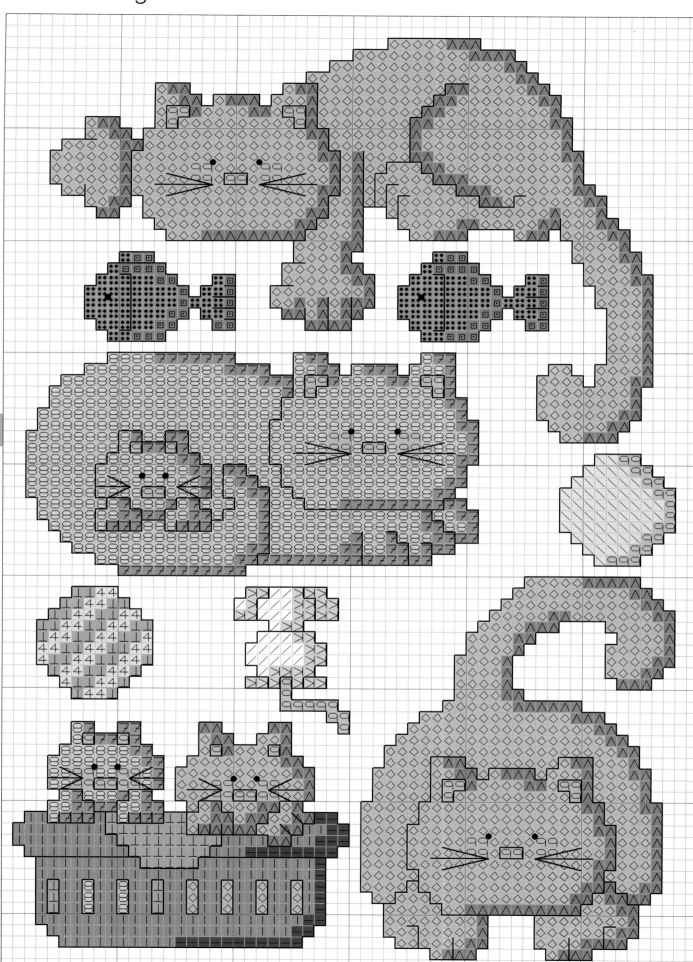

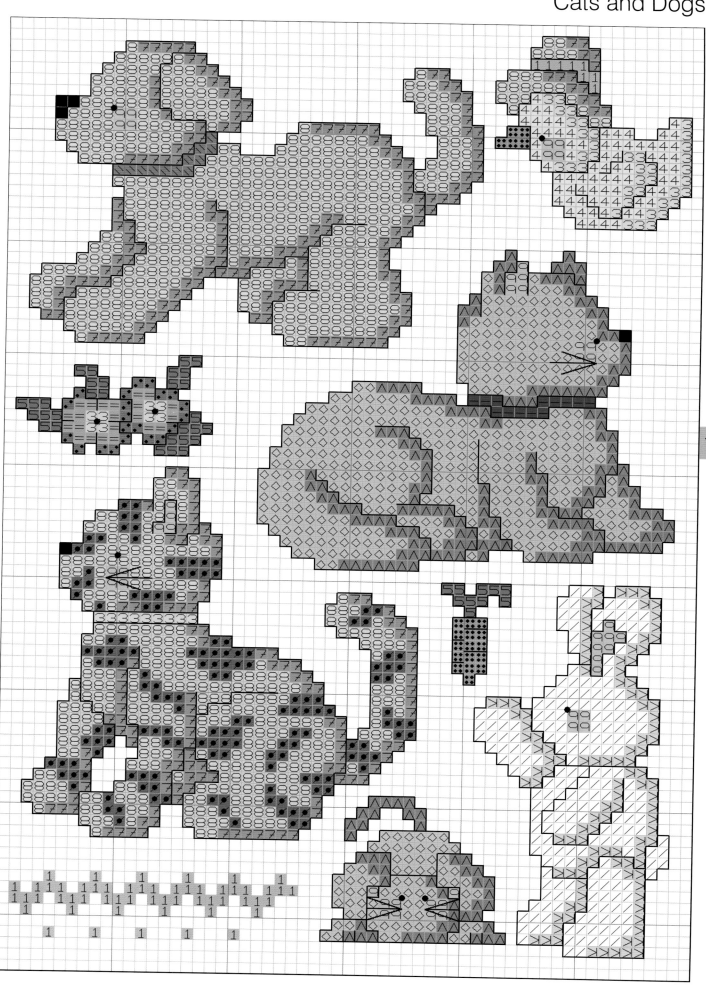

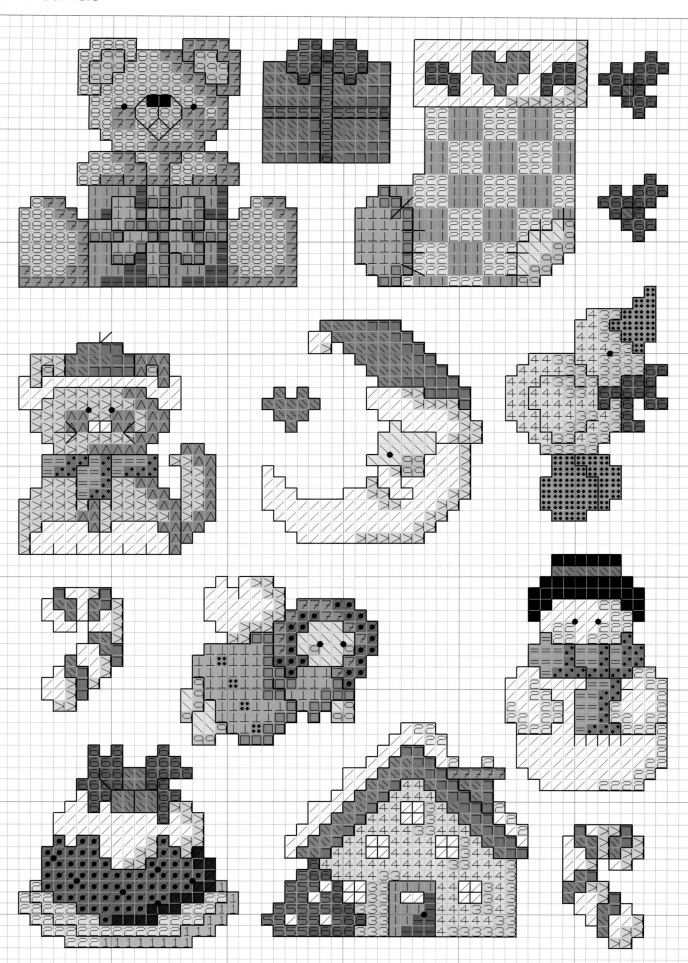

112

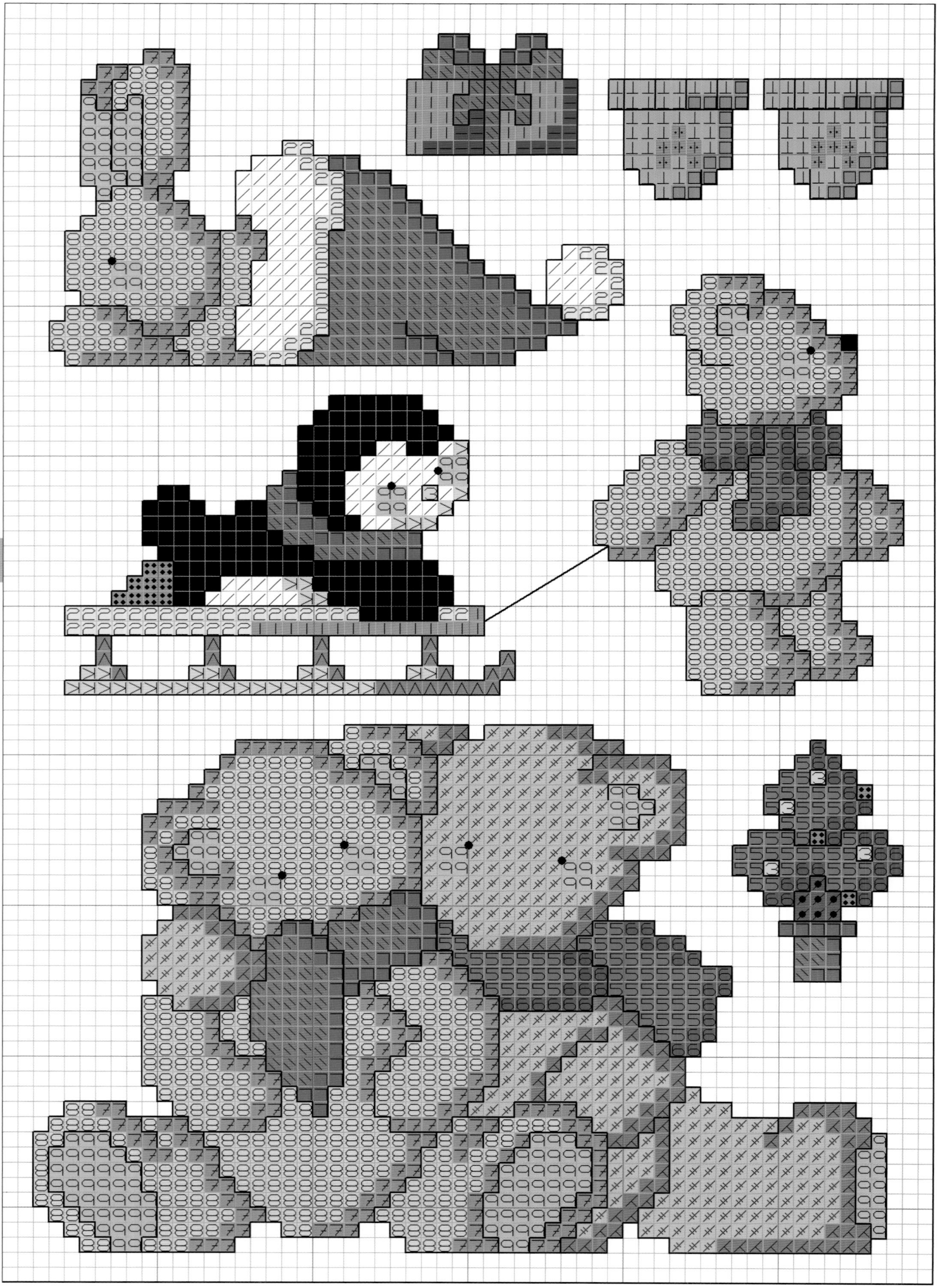

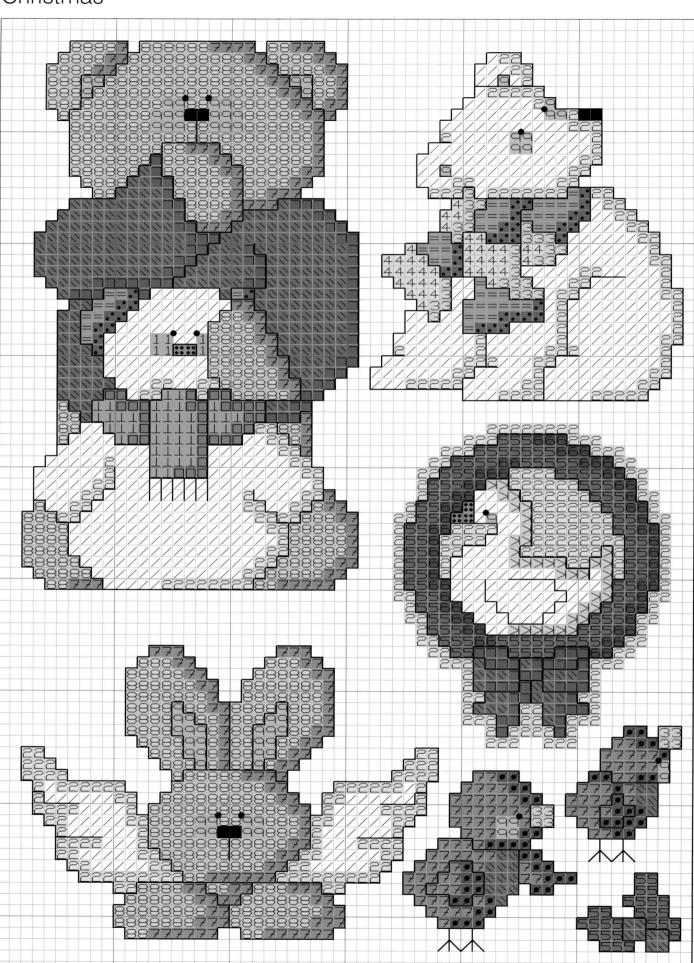

118

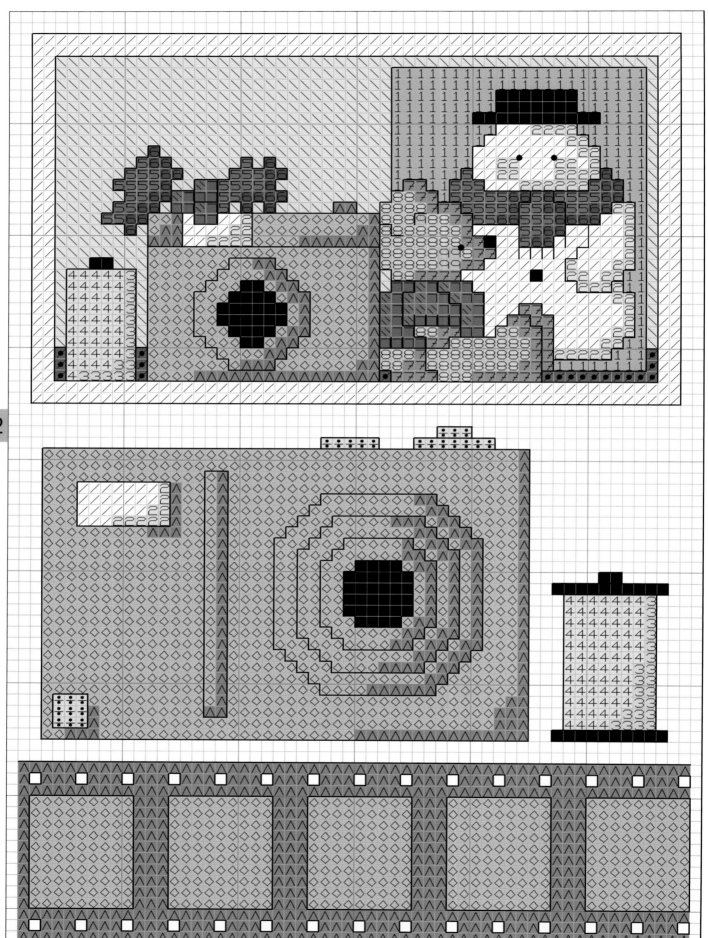

126

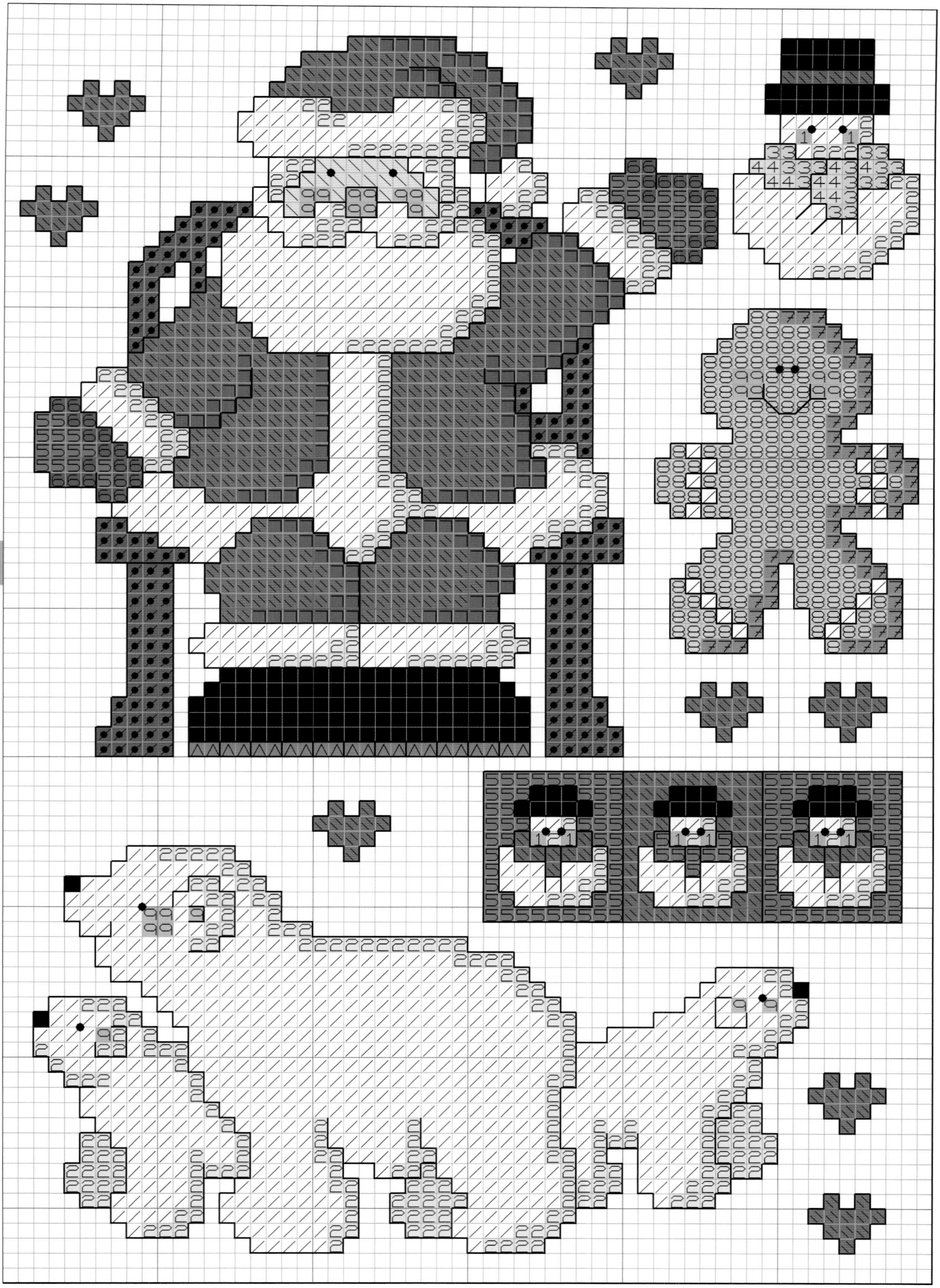

131

134

138

140

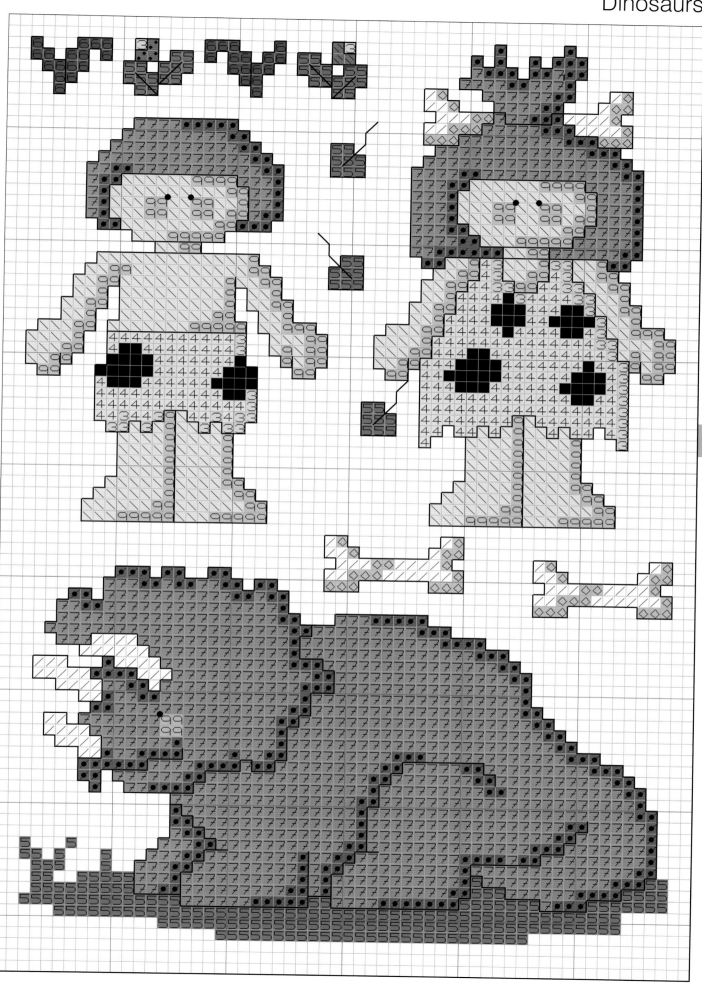

143

144

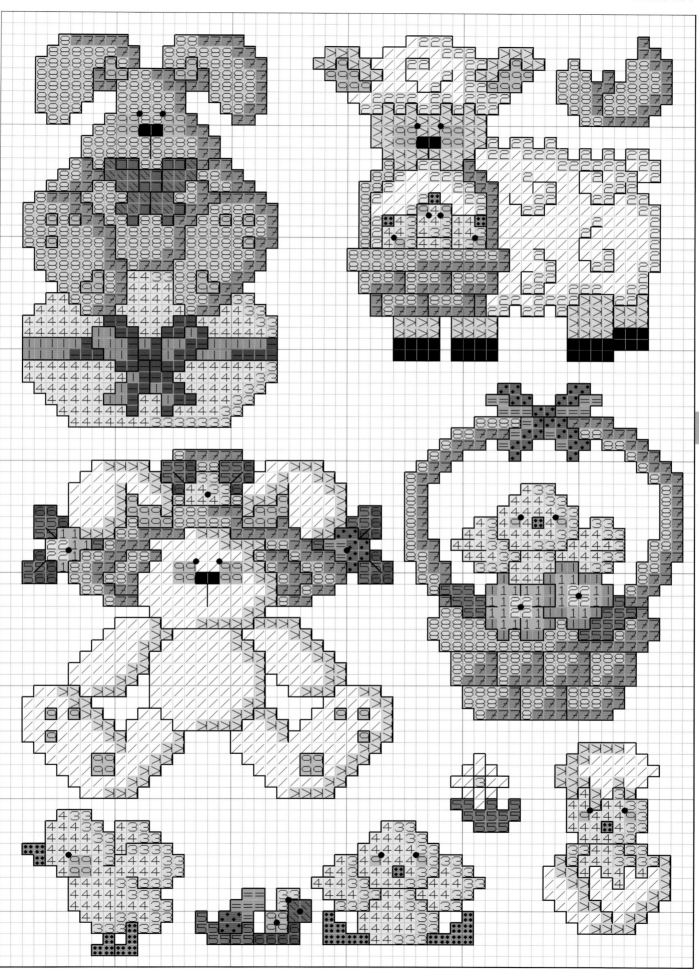

148

149

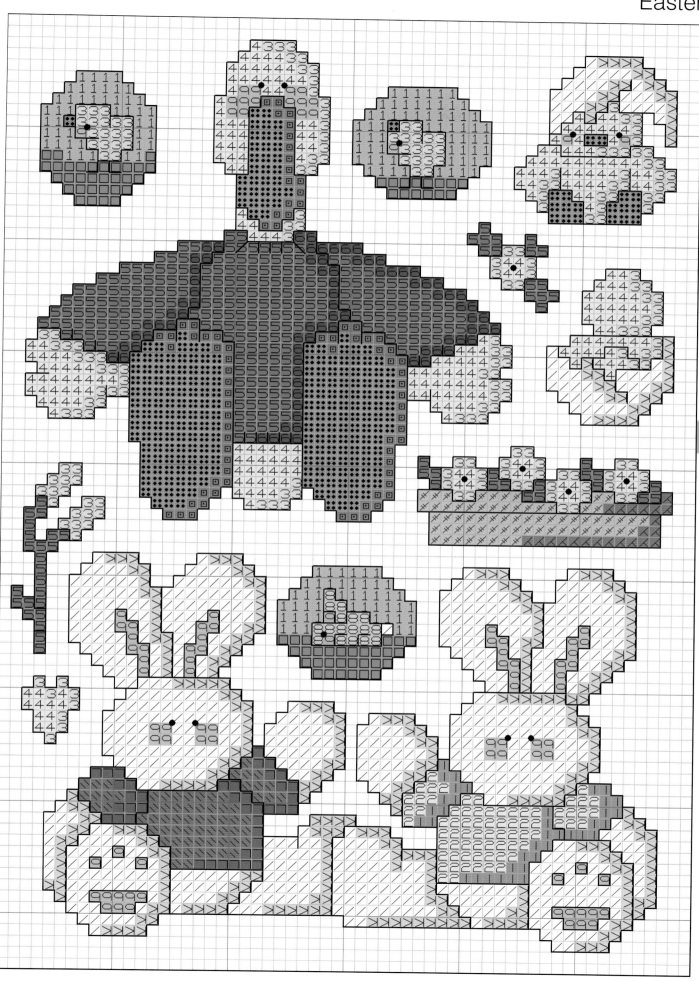

154

156

163

Gardens

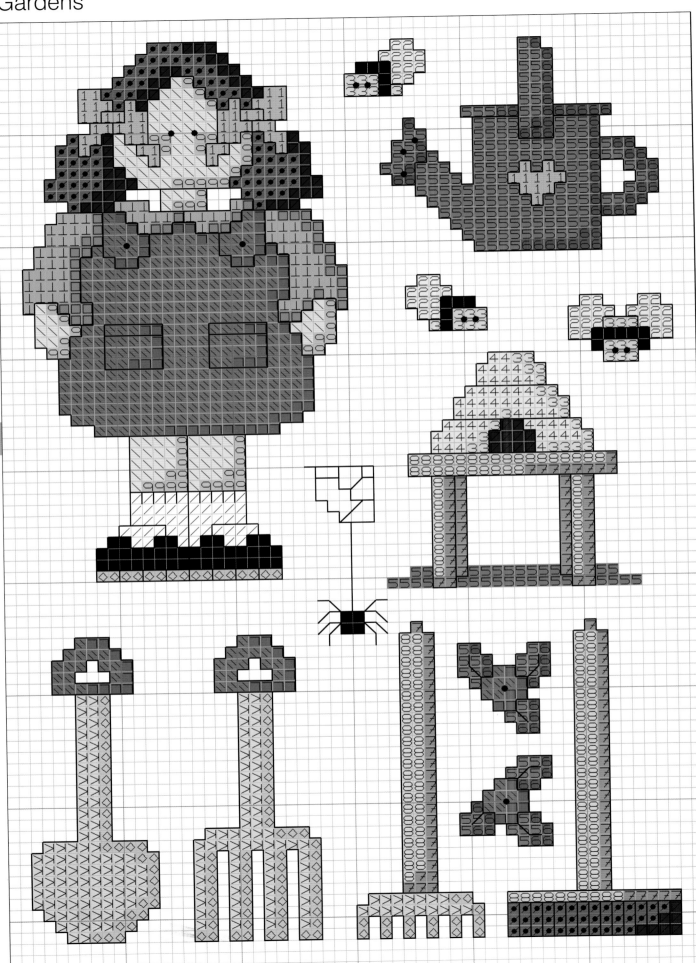

Gardens

168

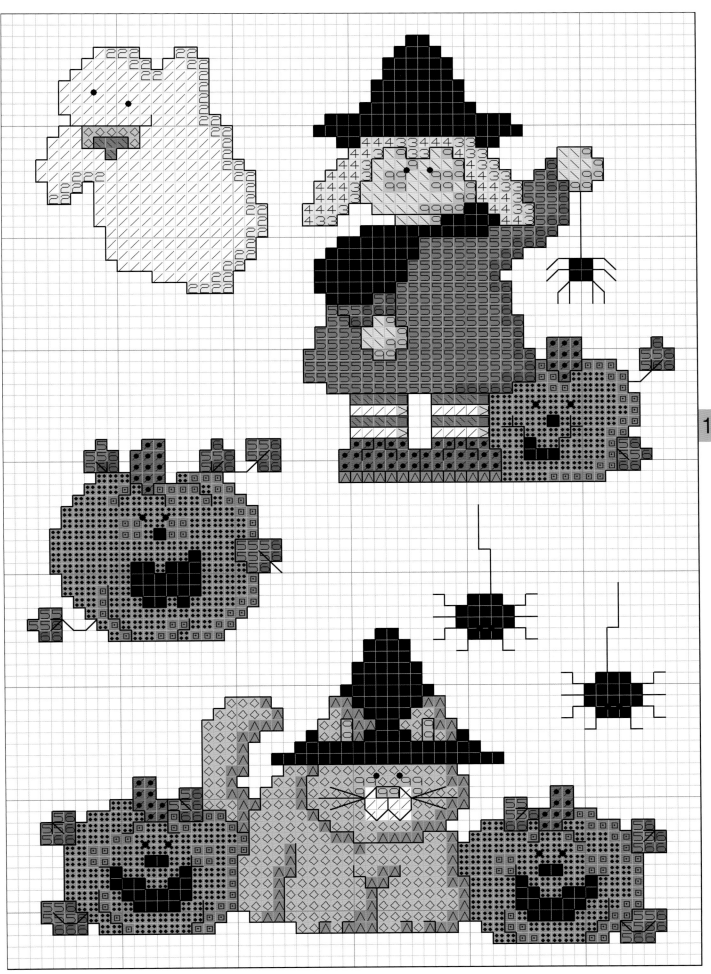

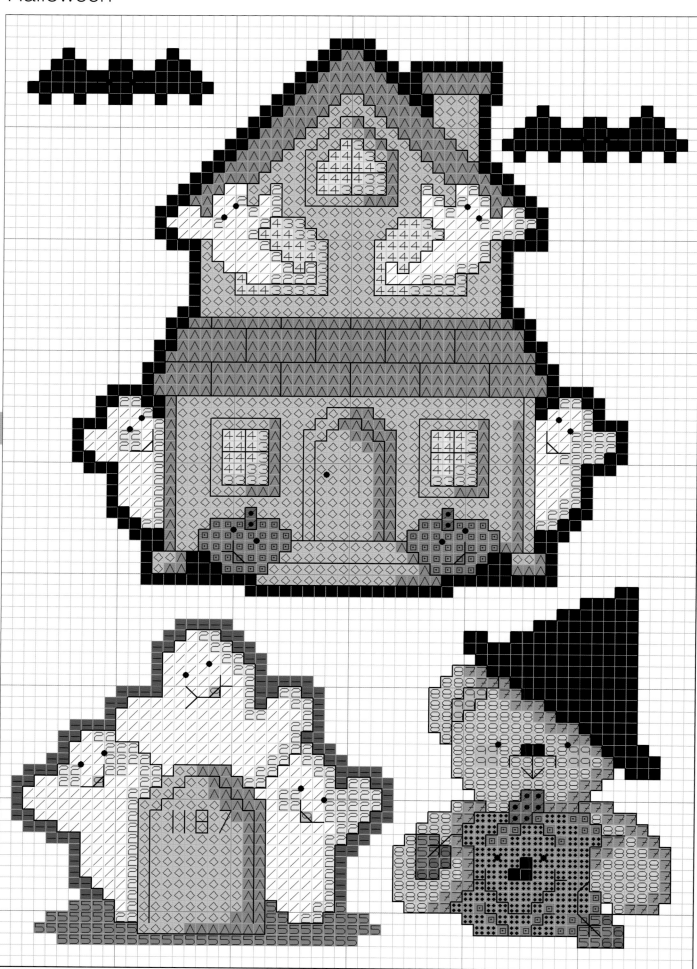

172

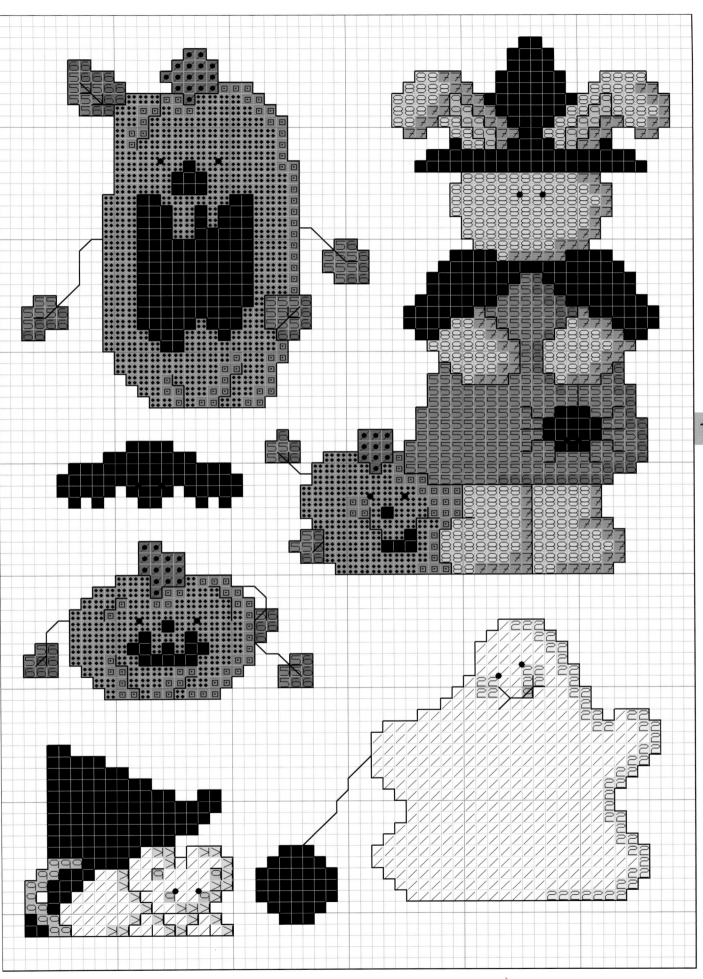

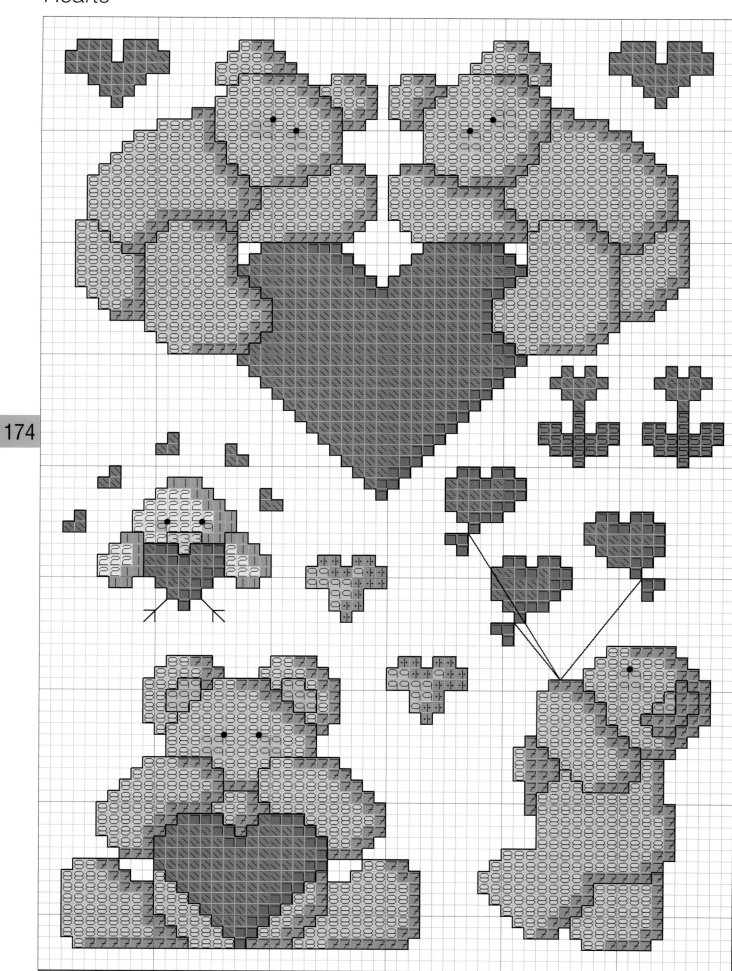

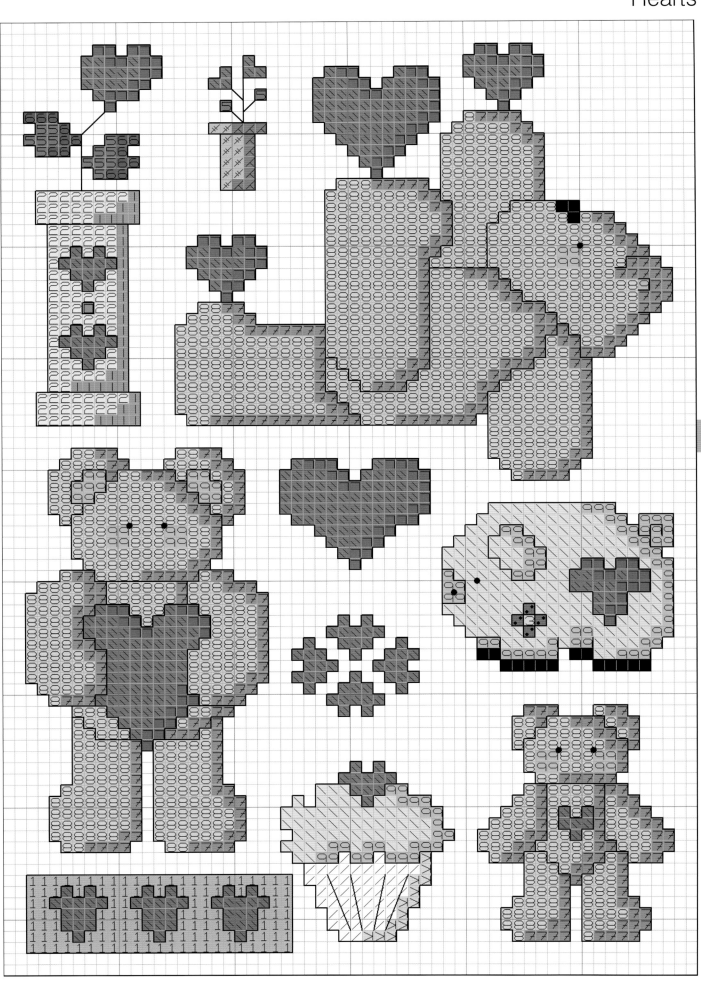

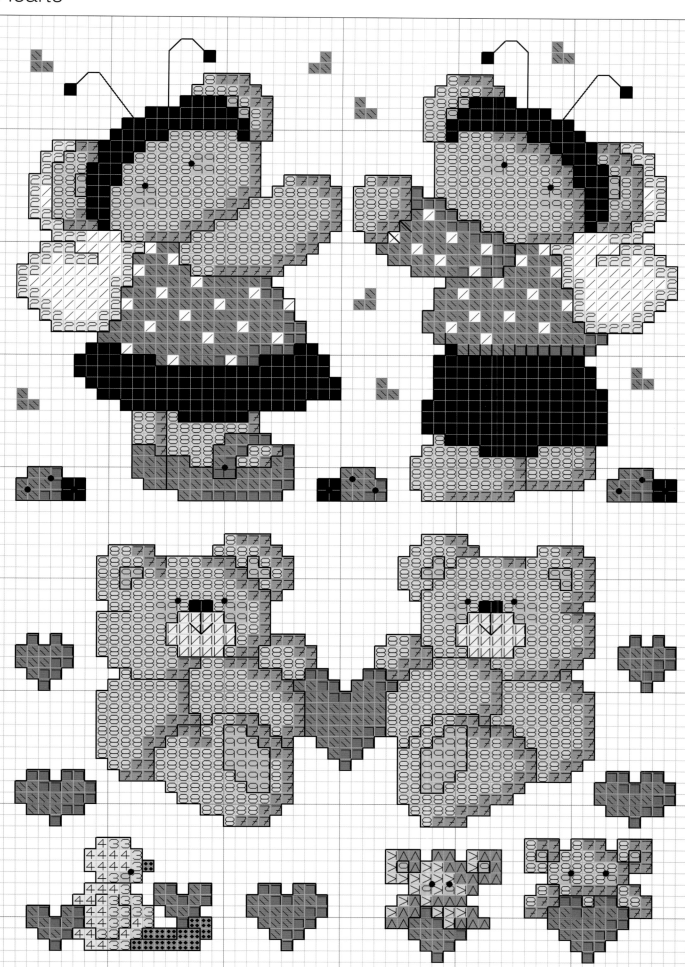

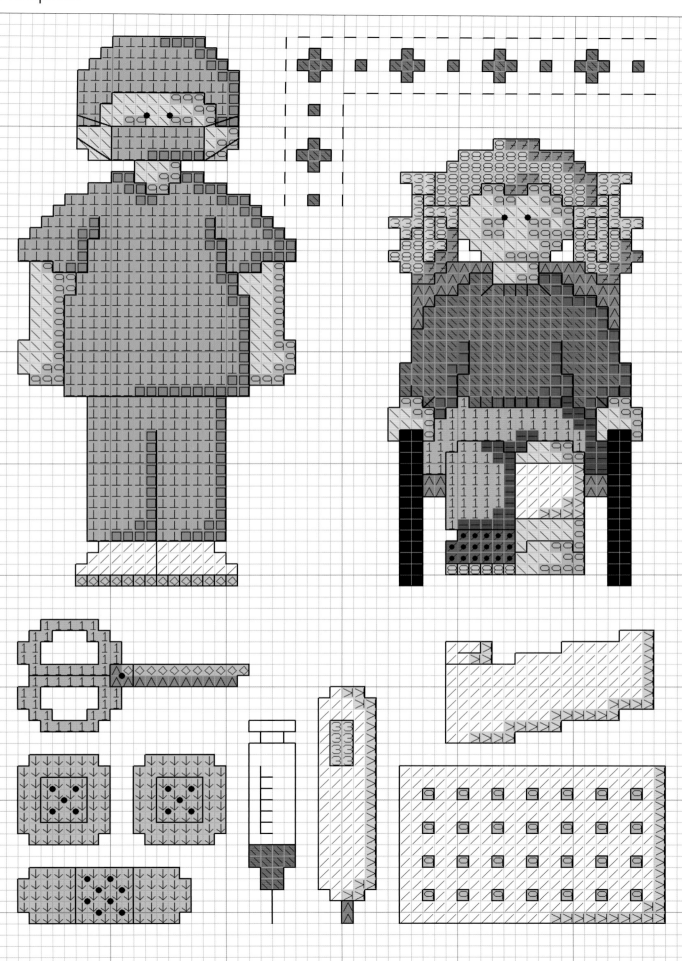

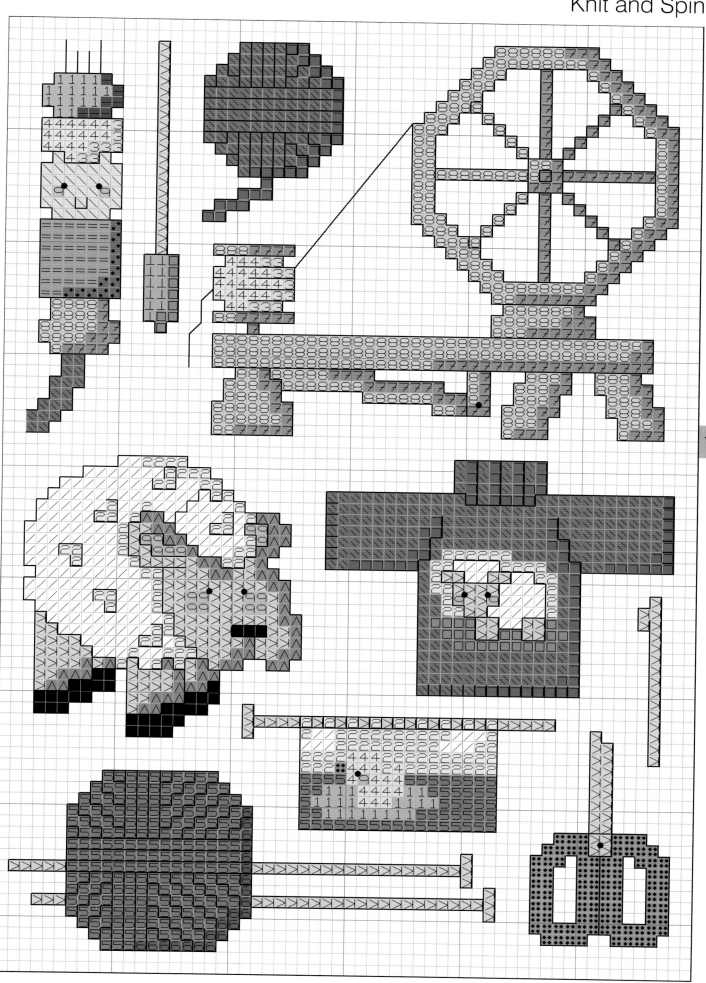

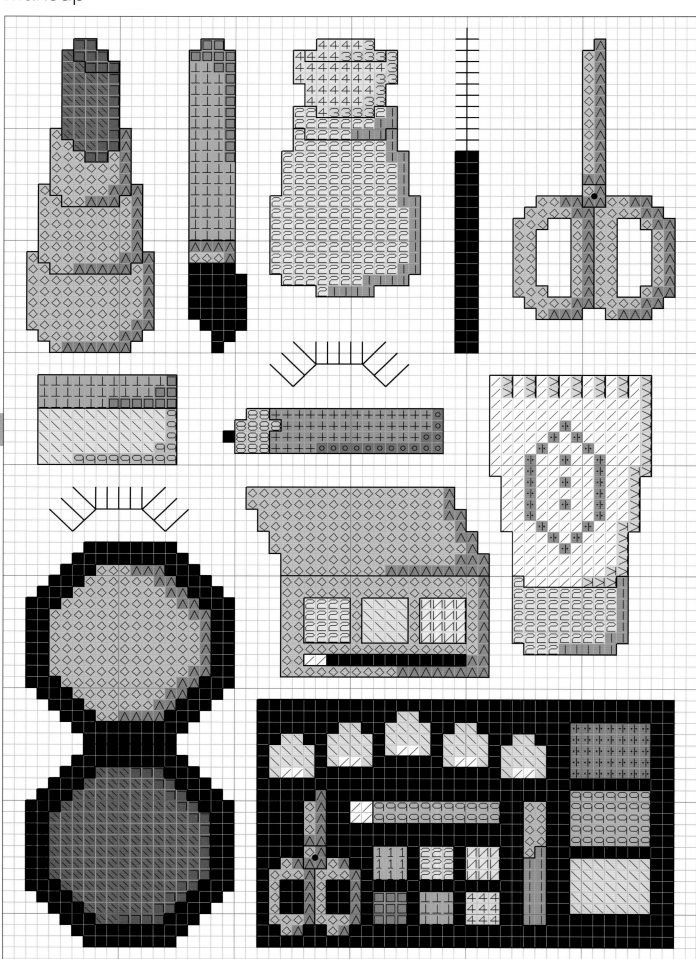

184

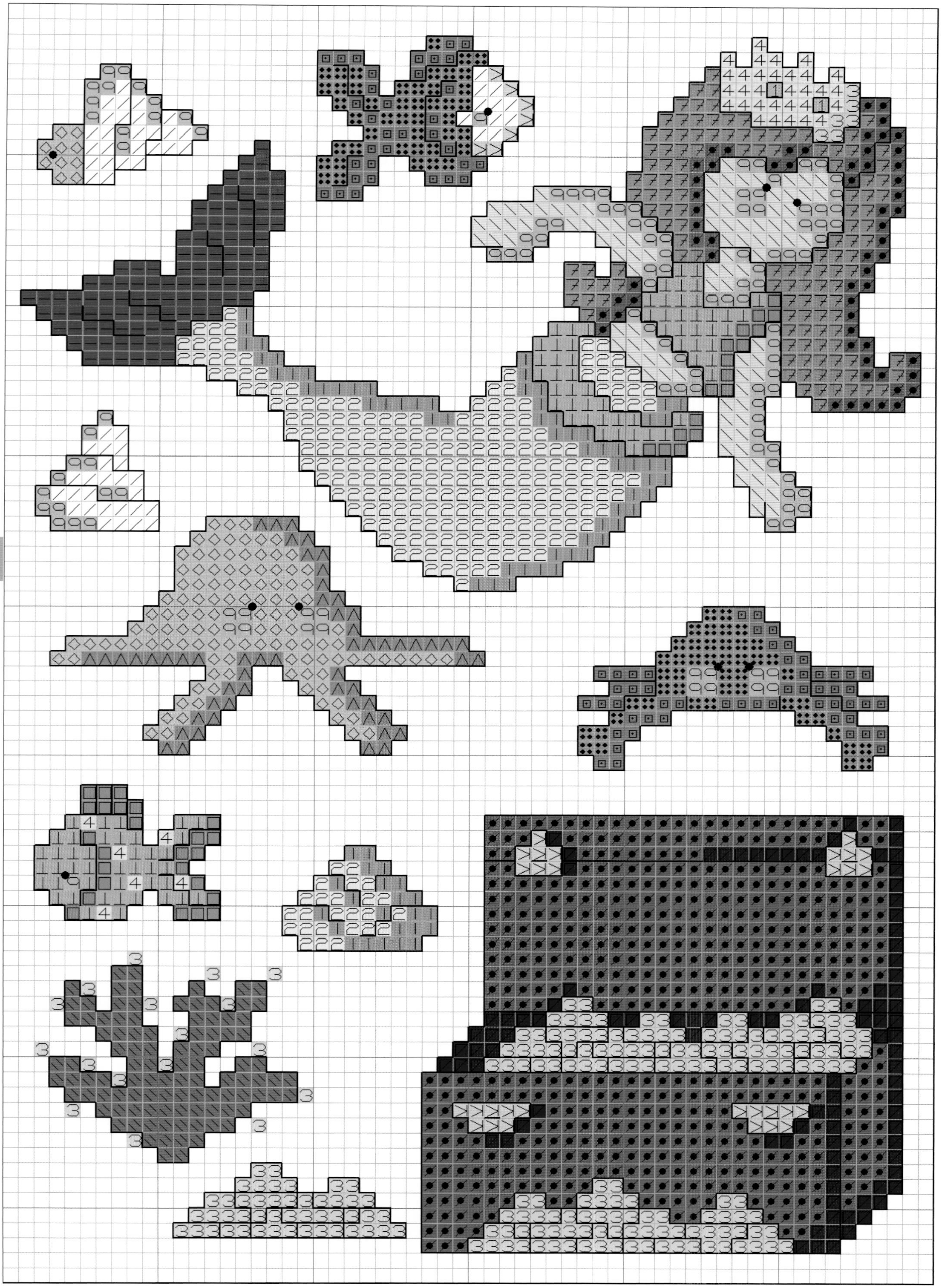

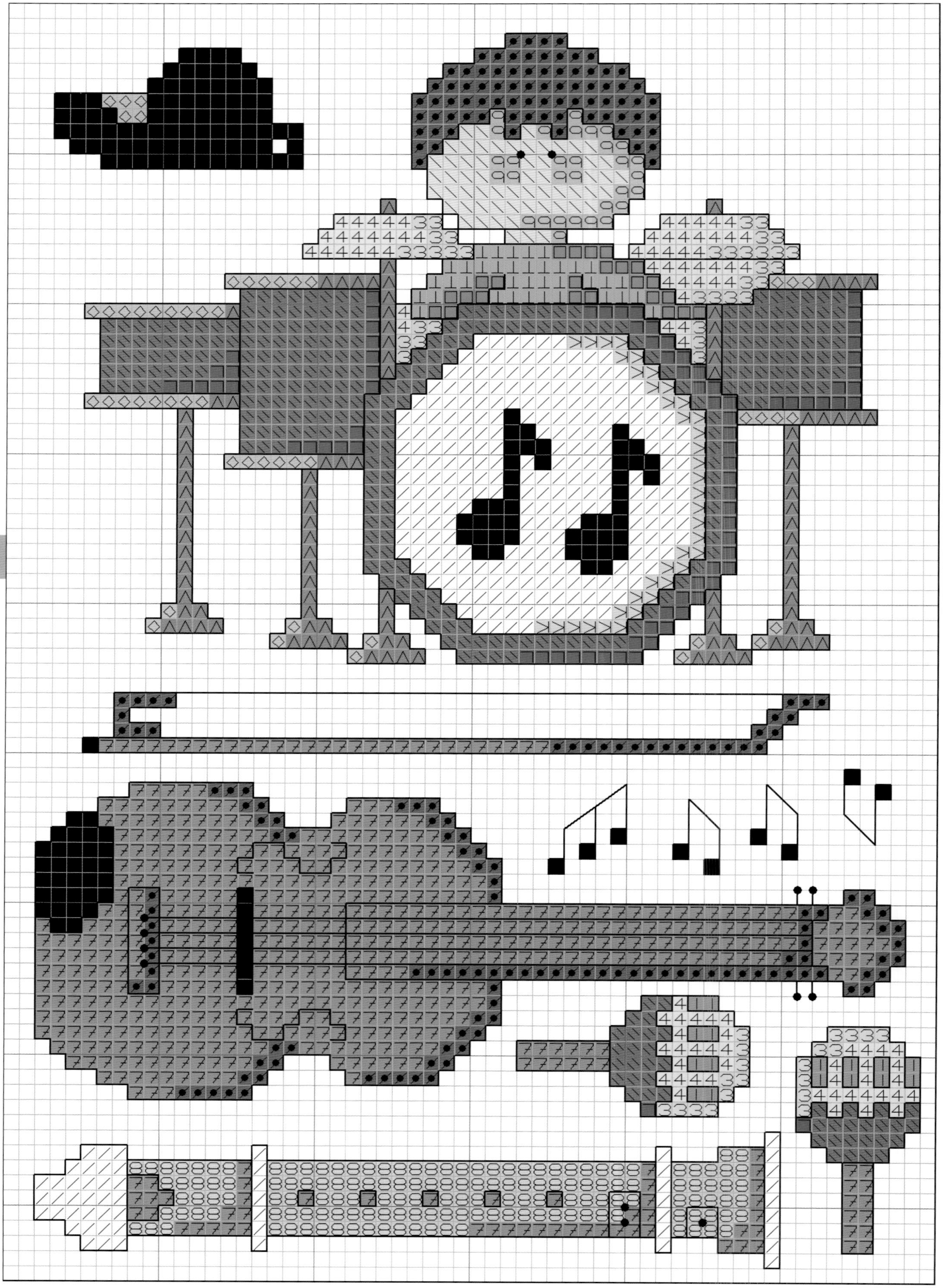

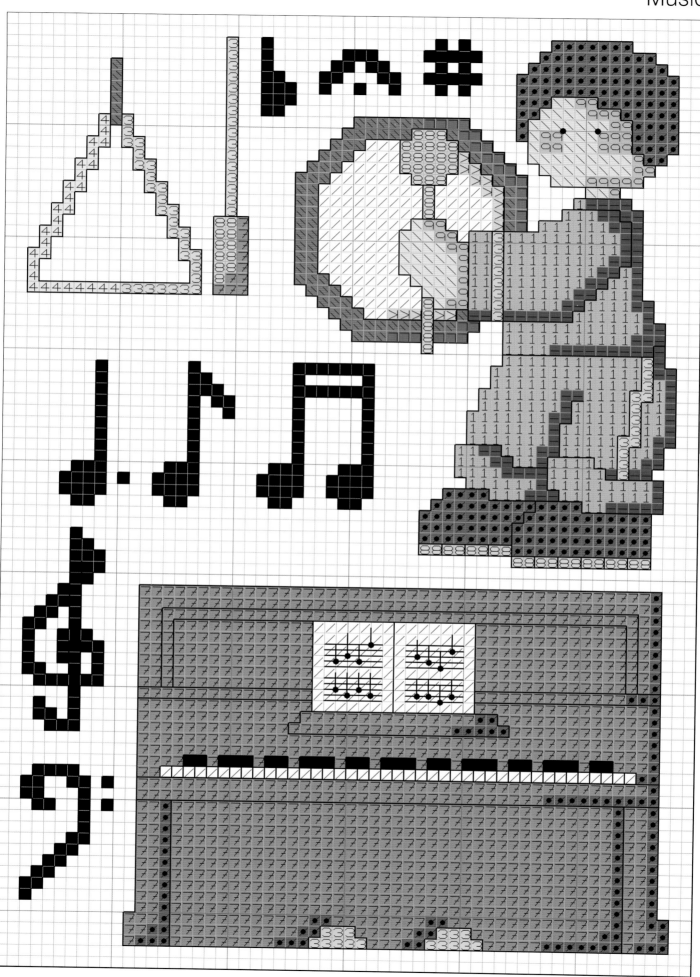

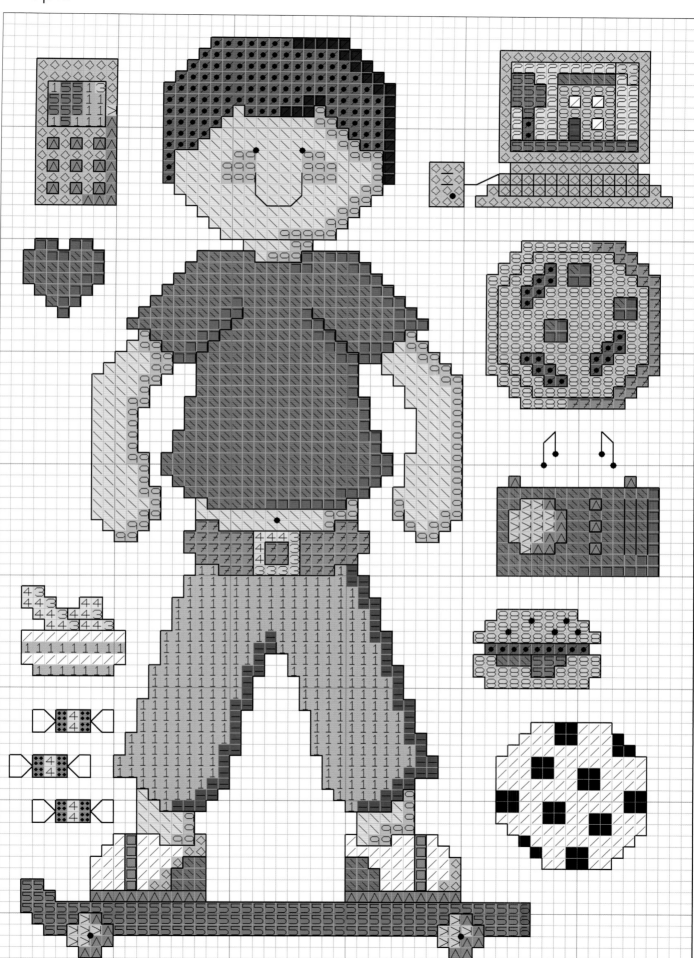

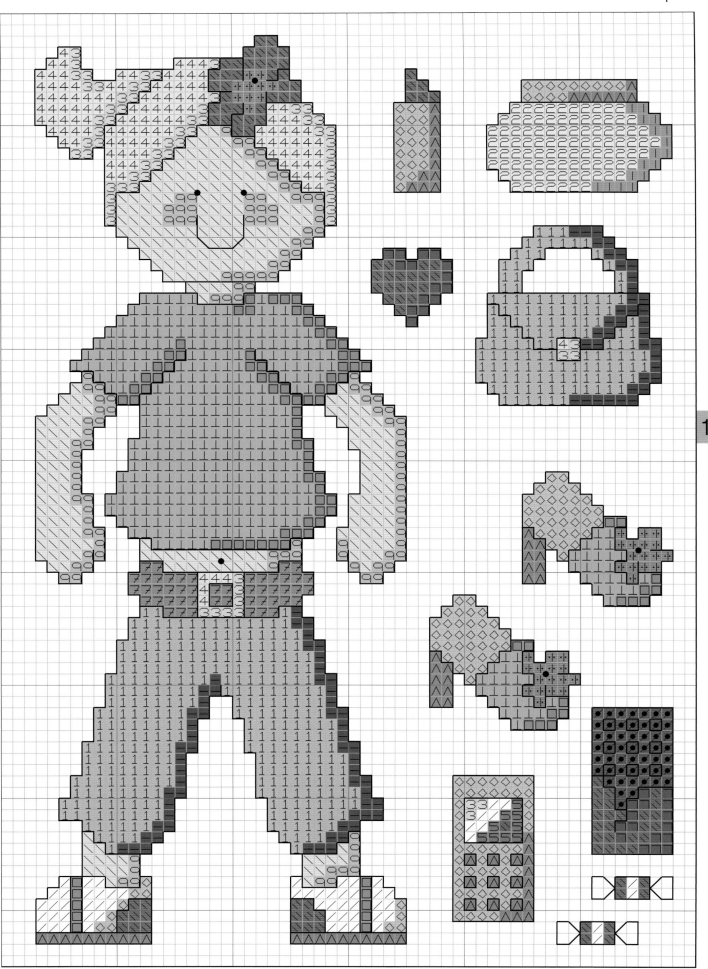

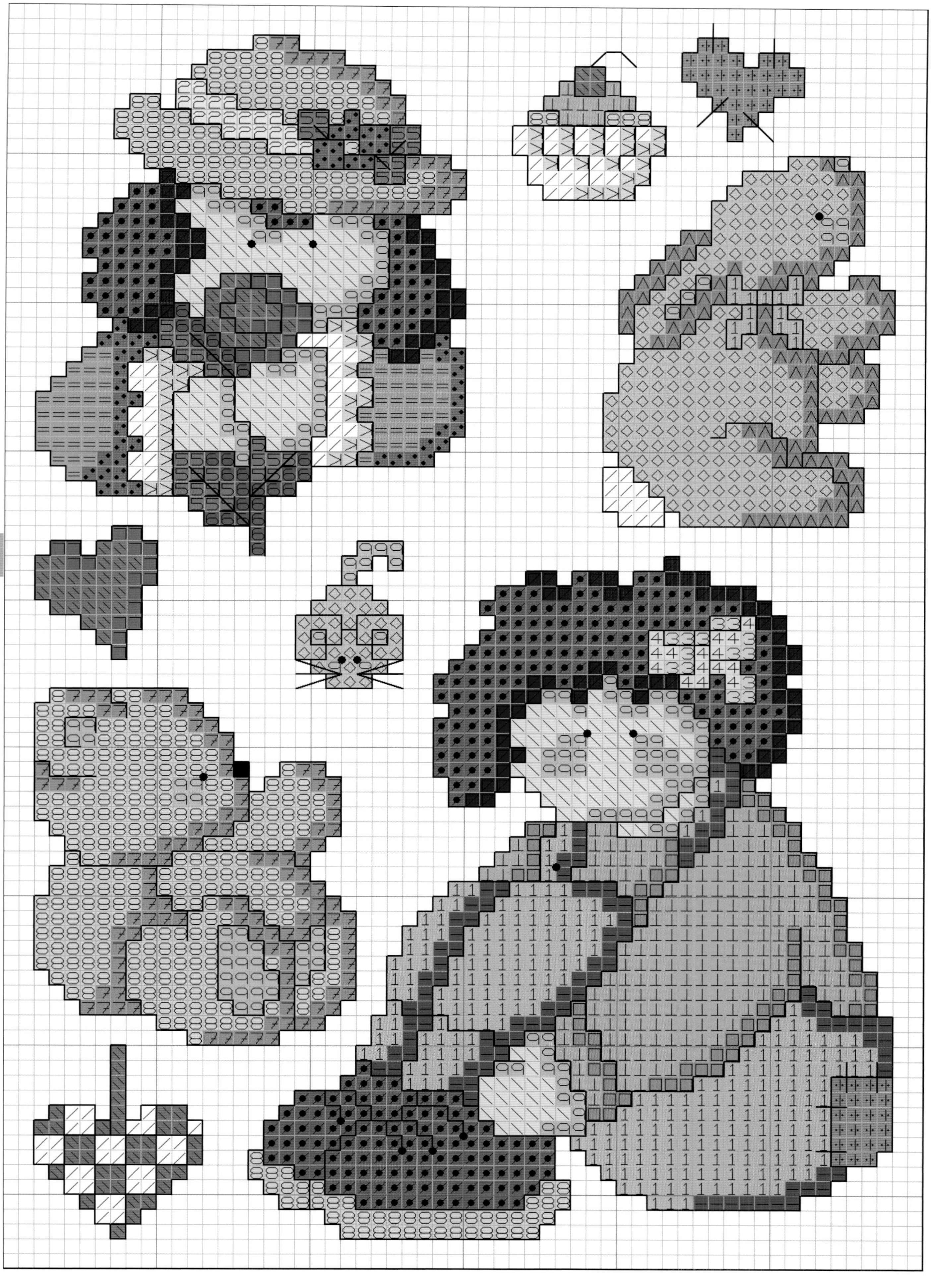

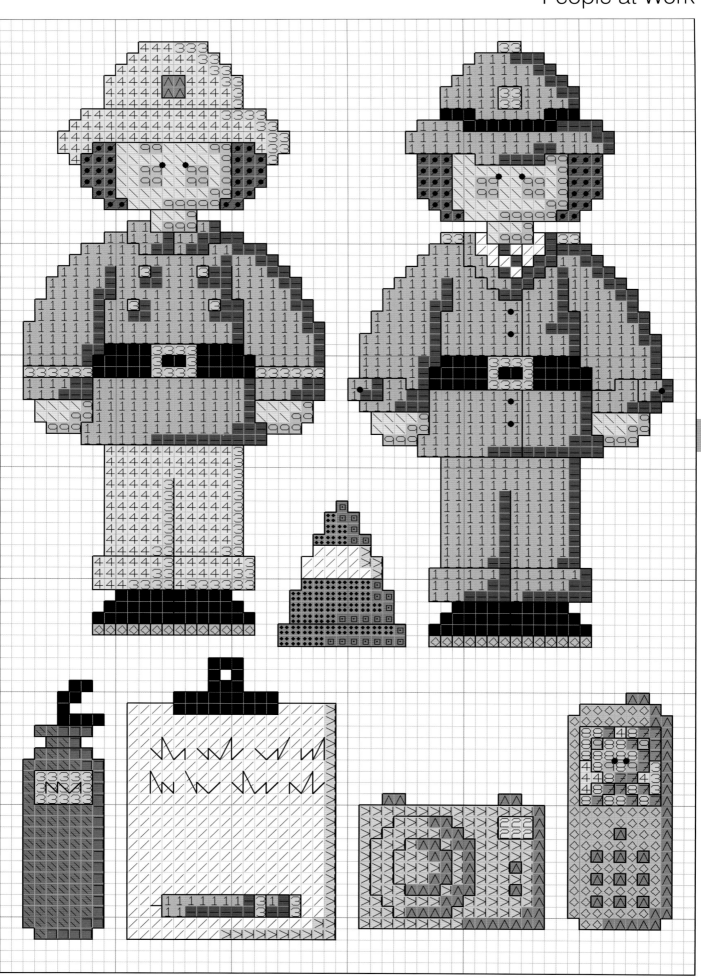

194

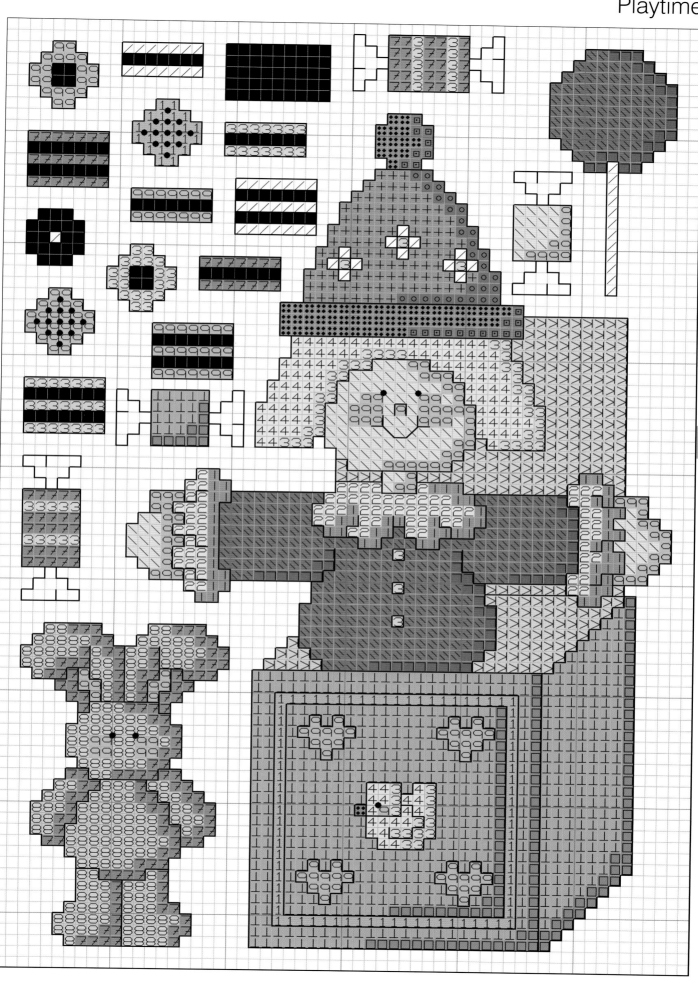

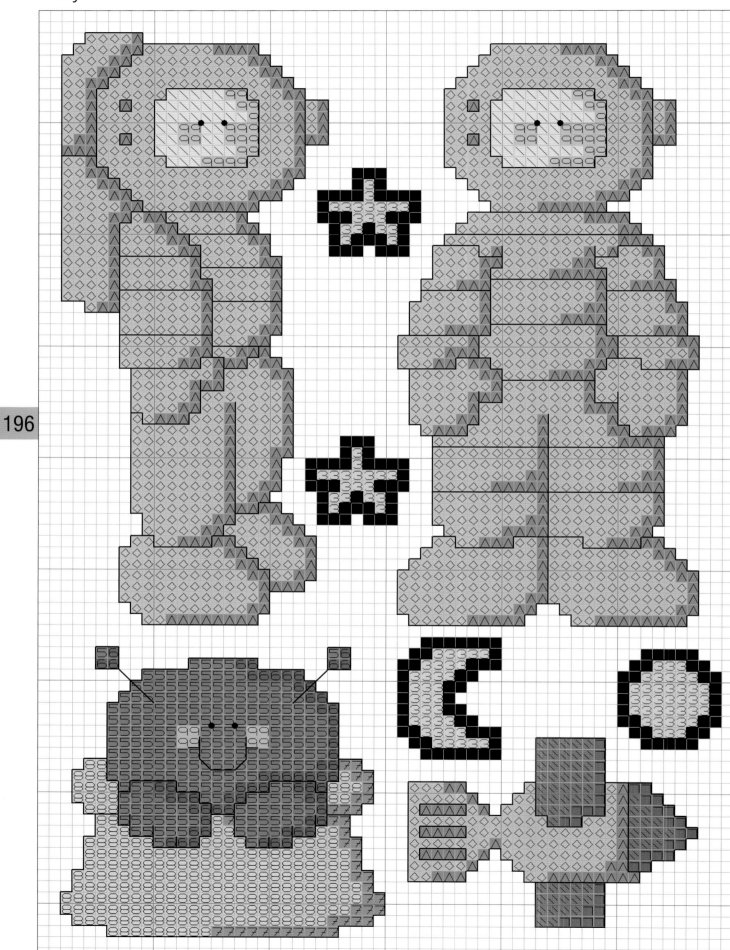

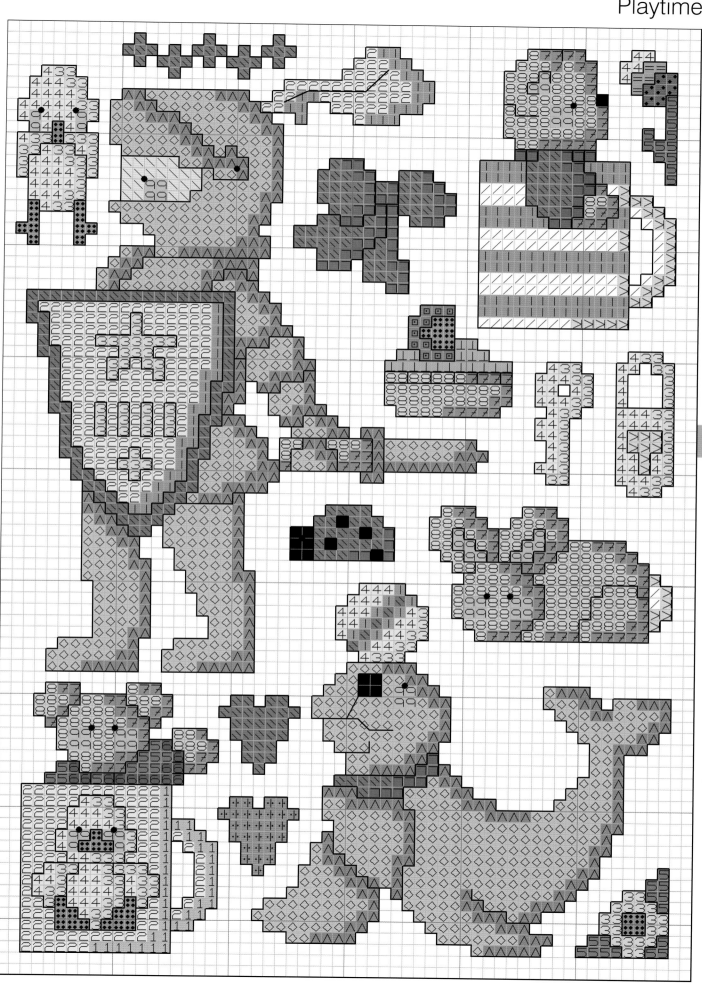

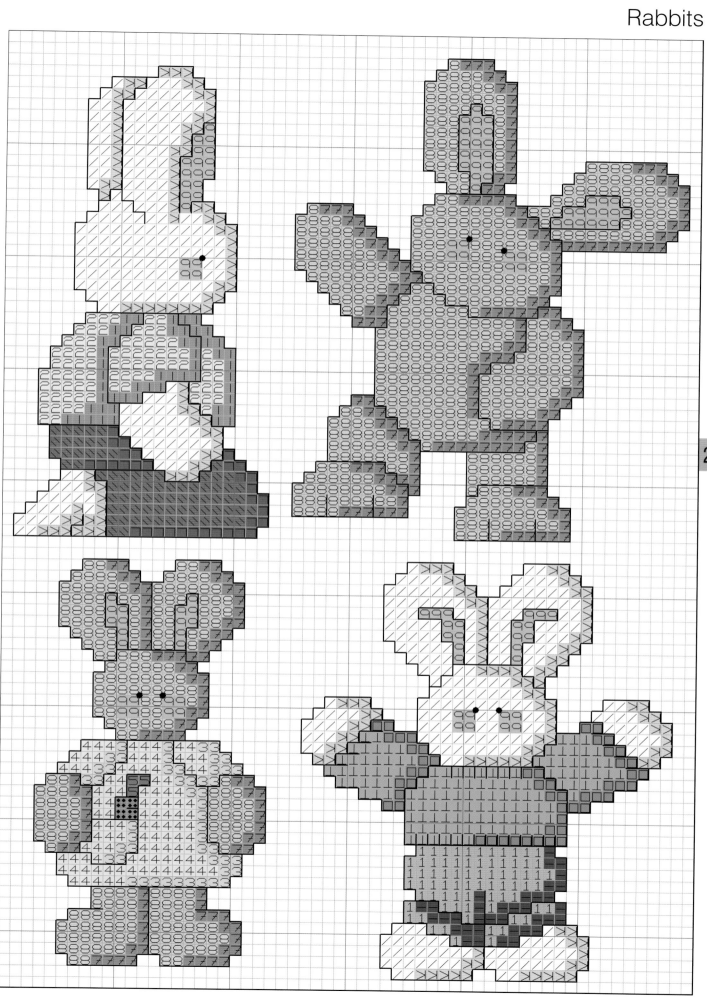

211

213

214

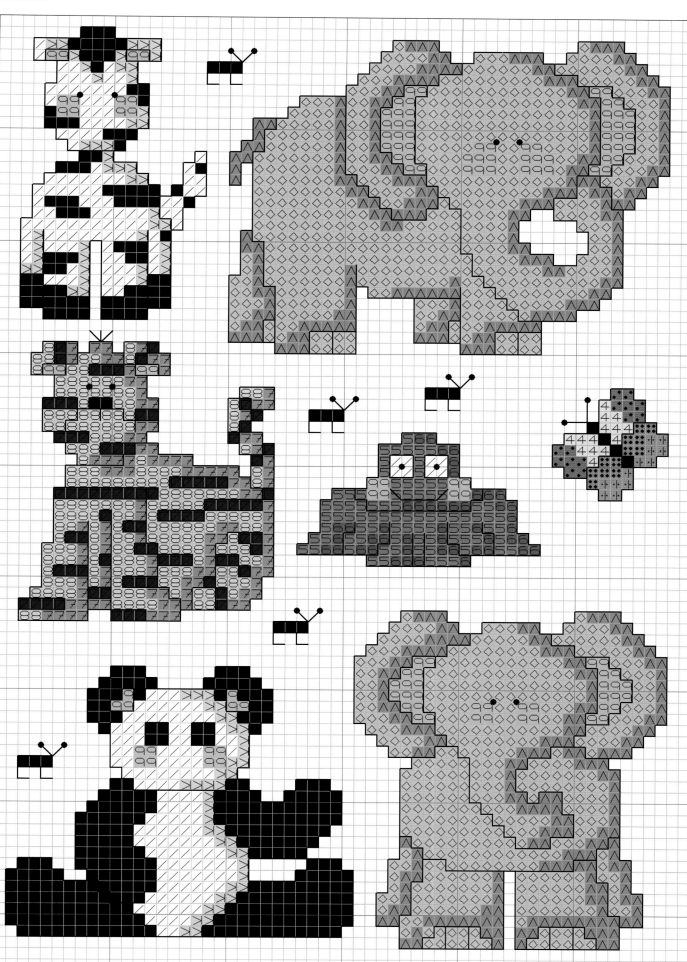

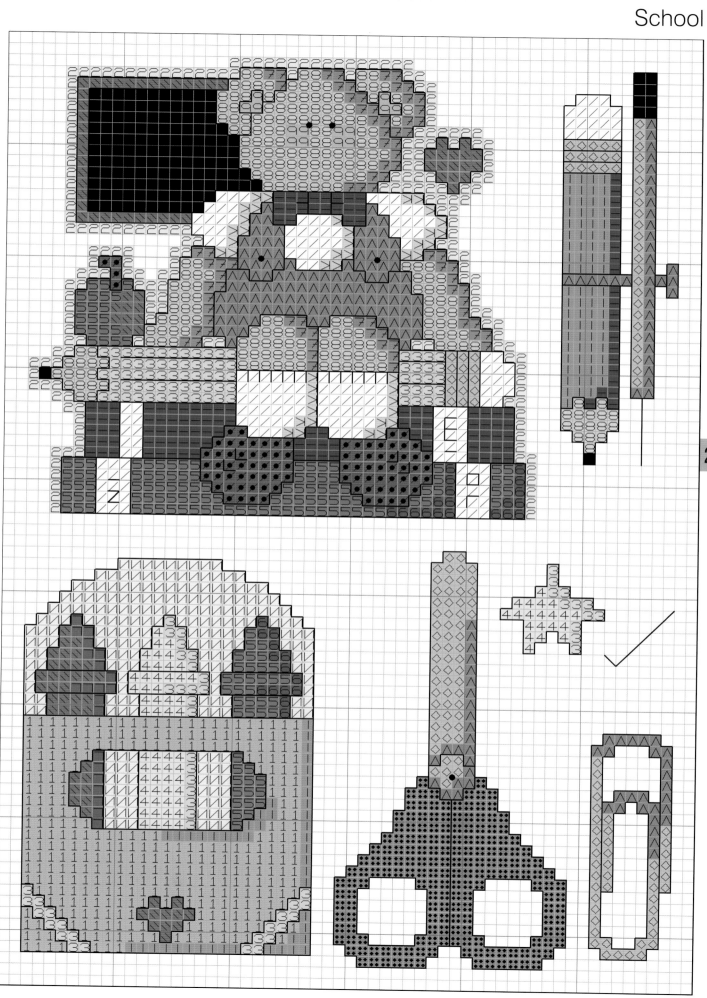

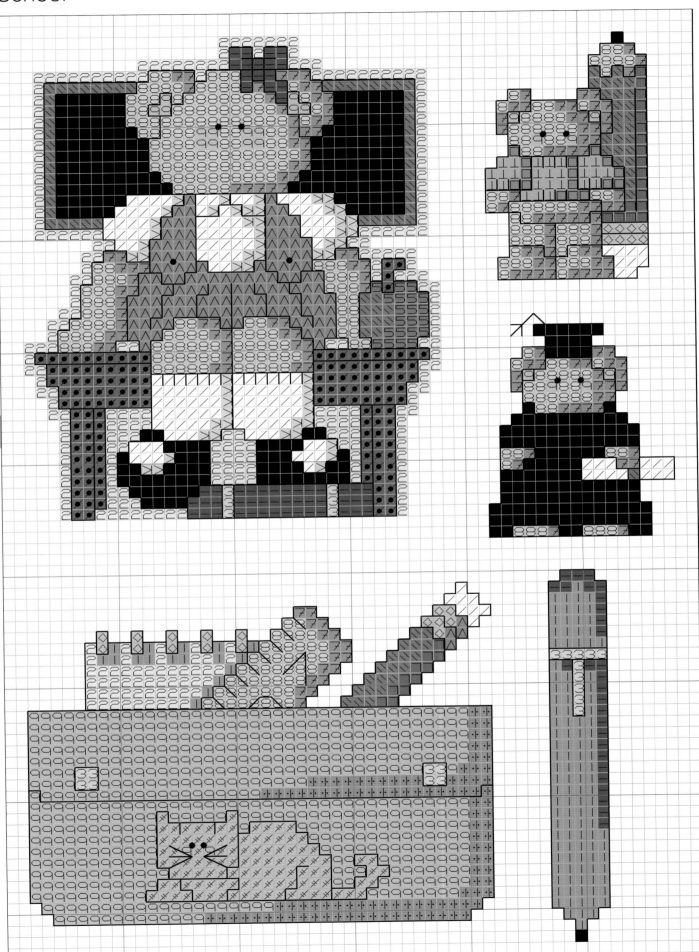

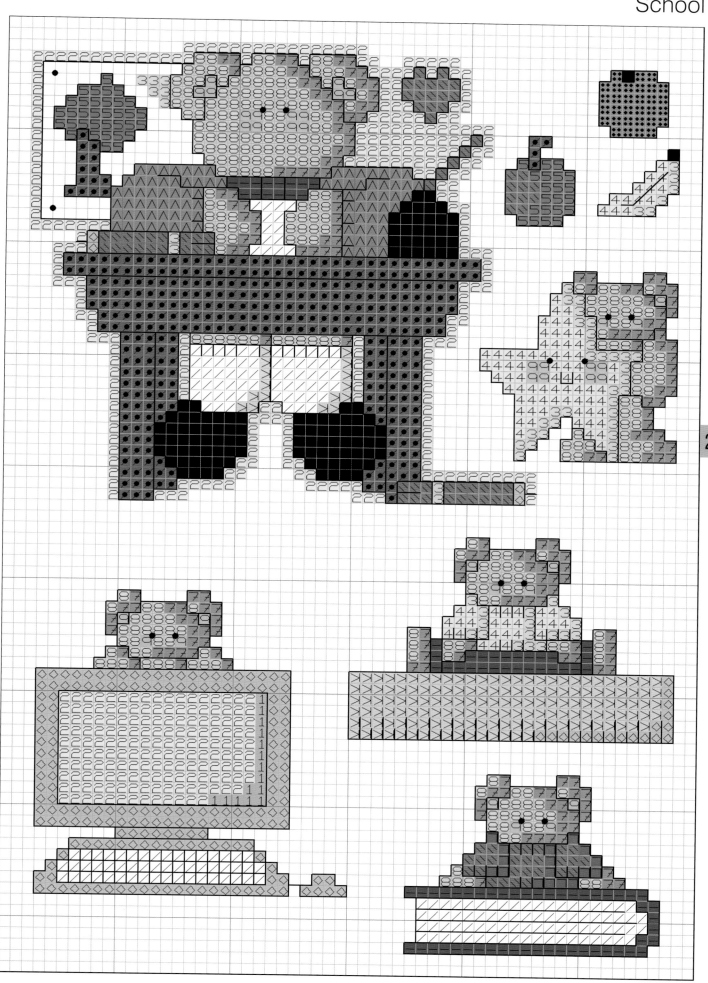

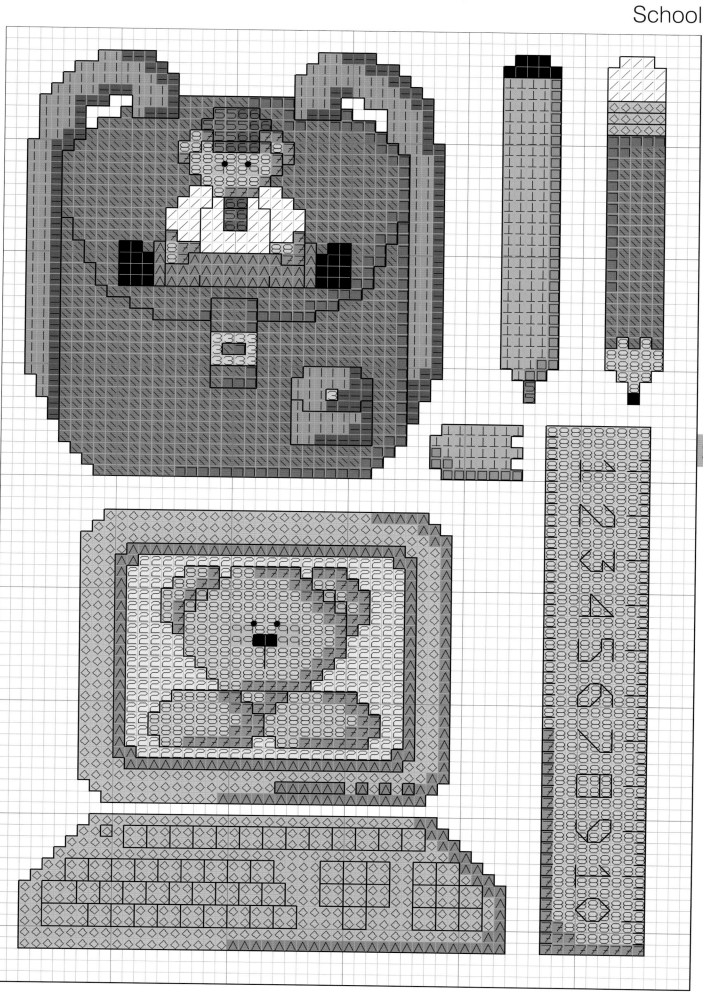

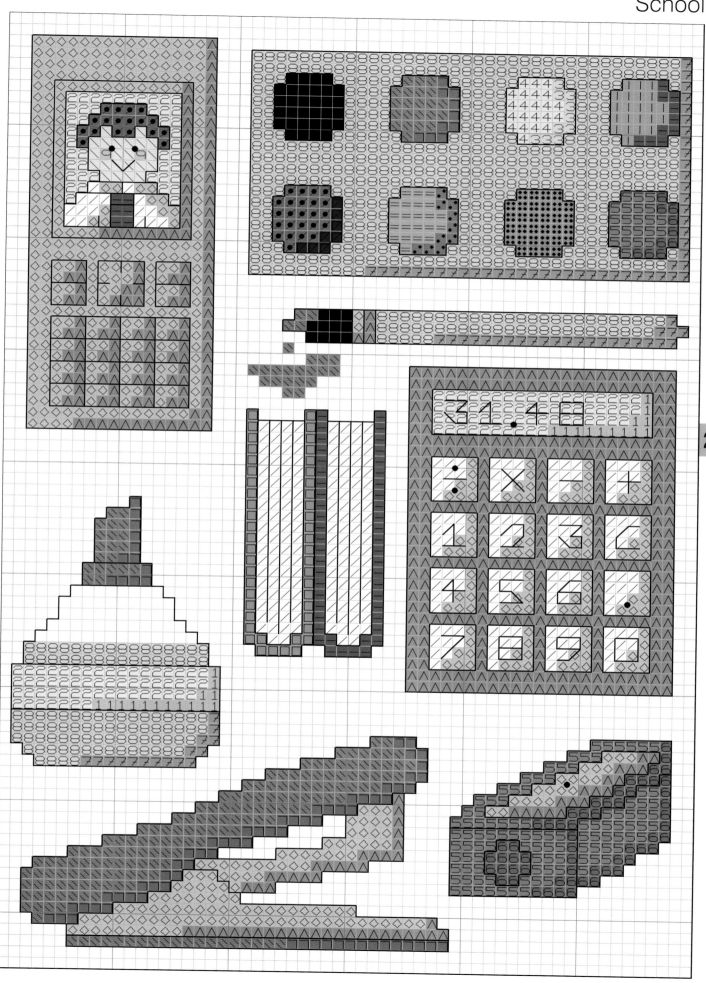

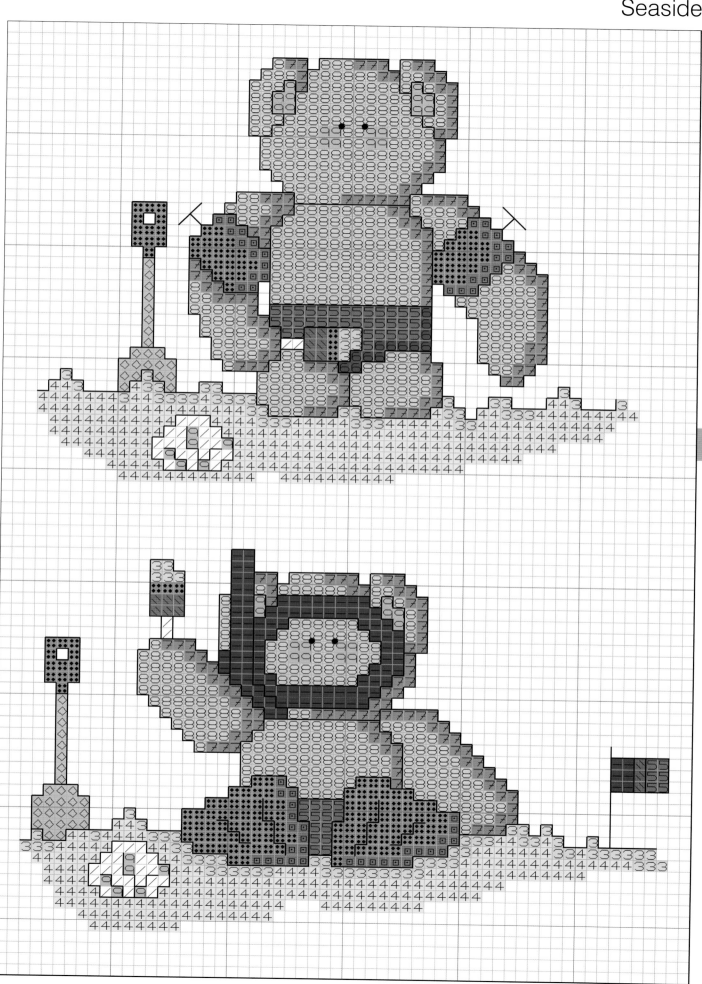

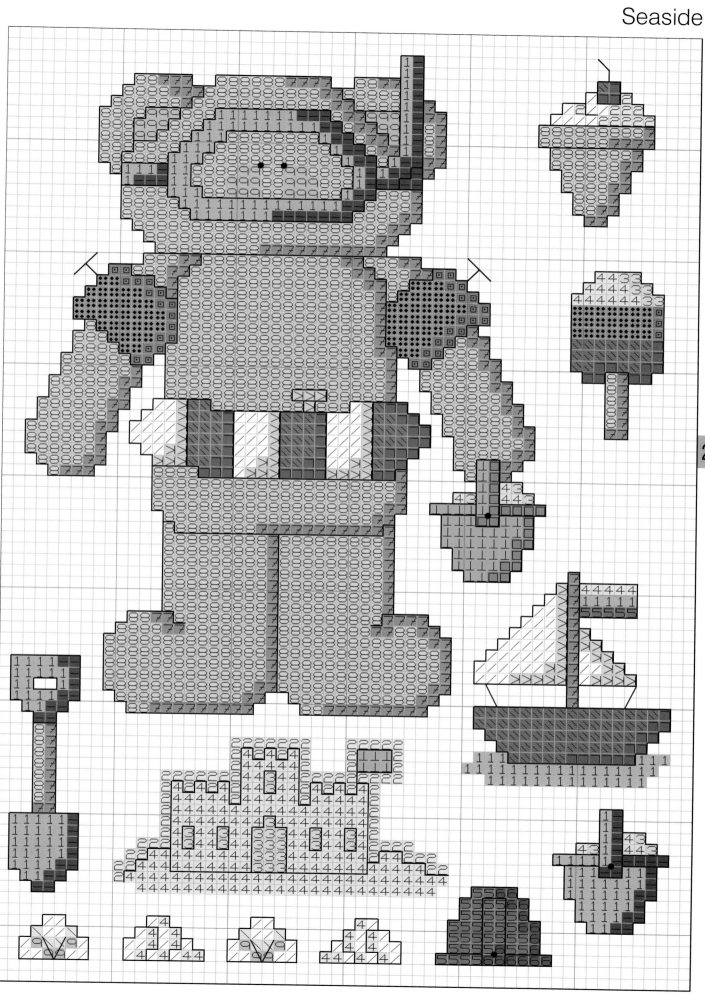

Seaside

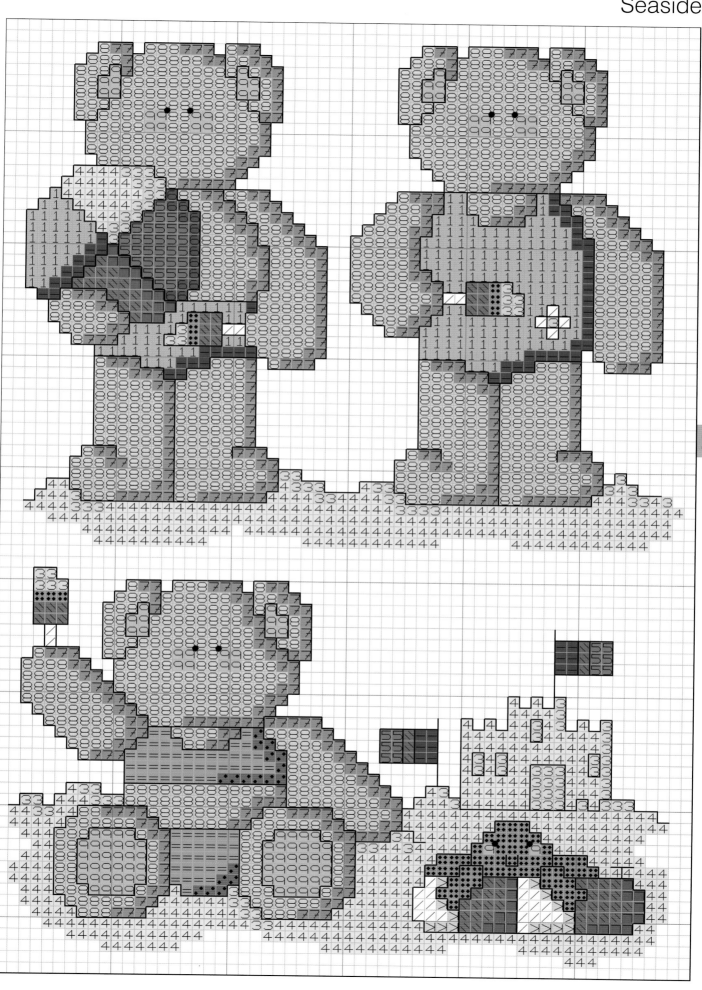

229

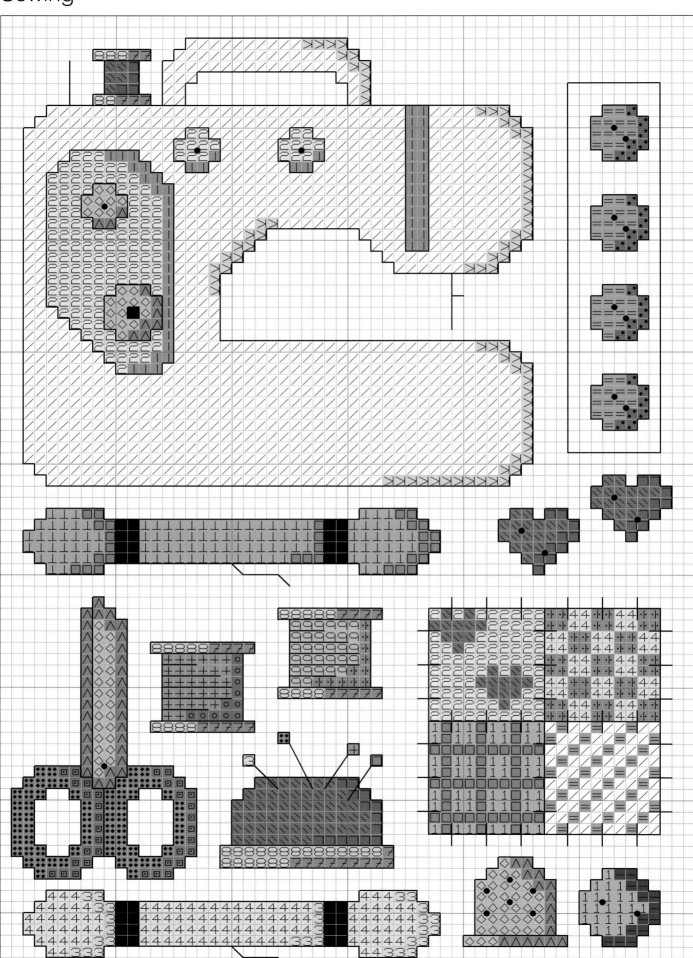

234

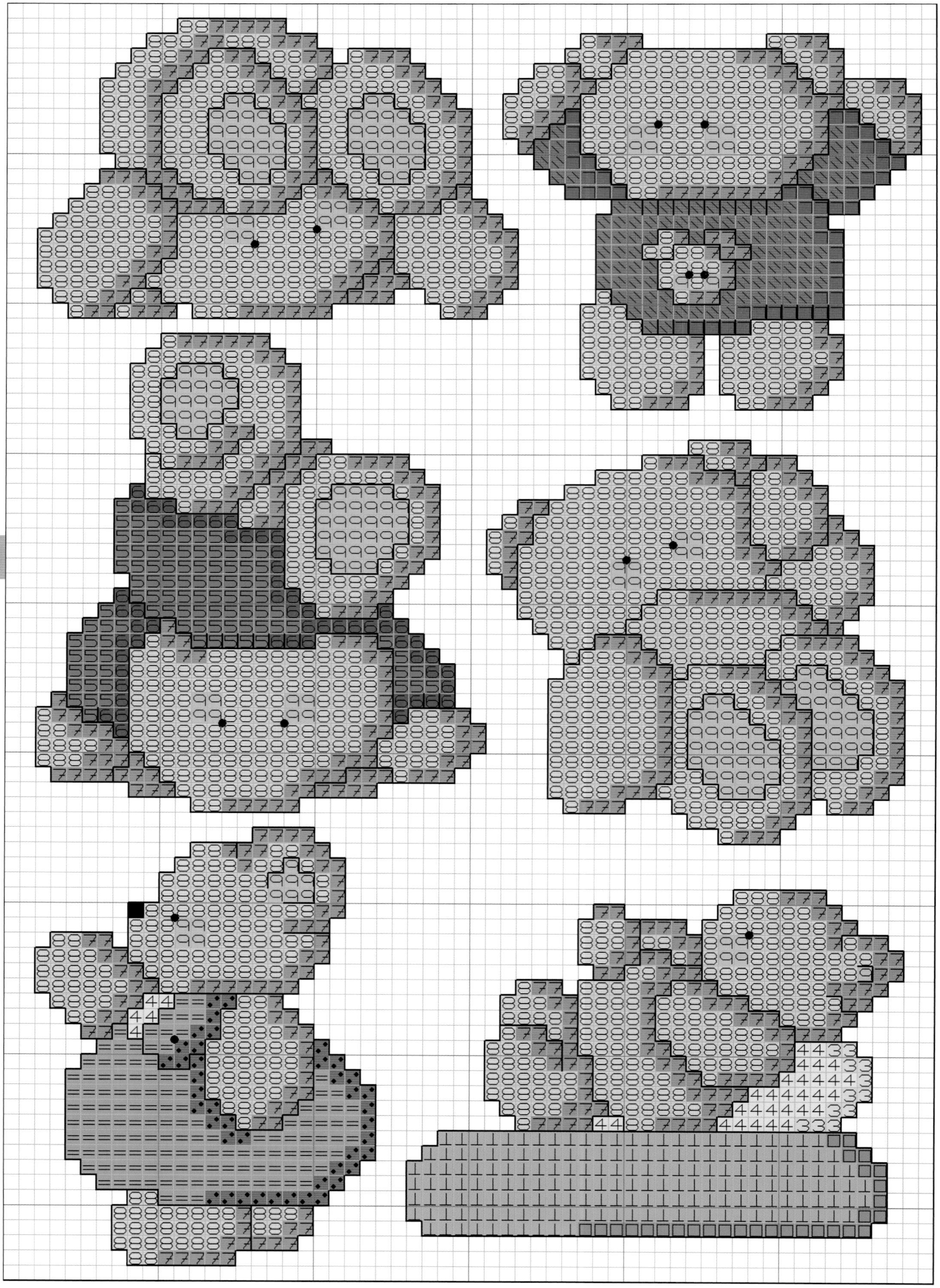

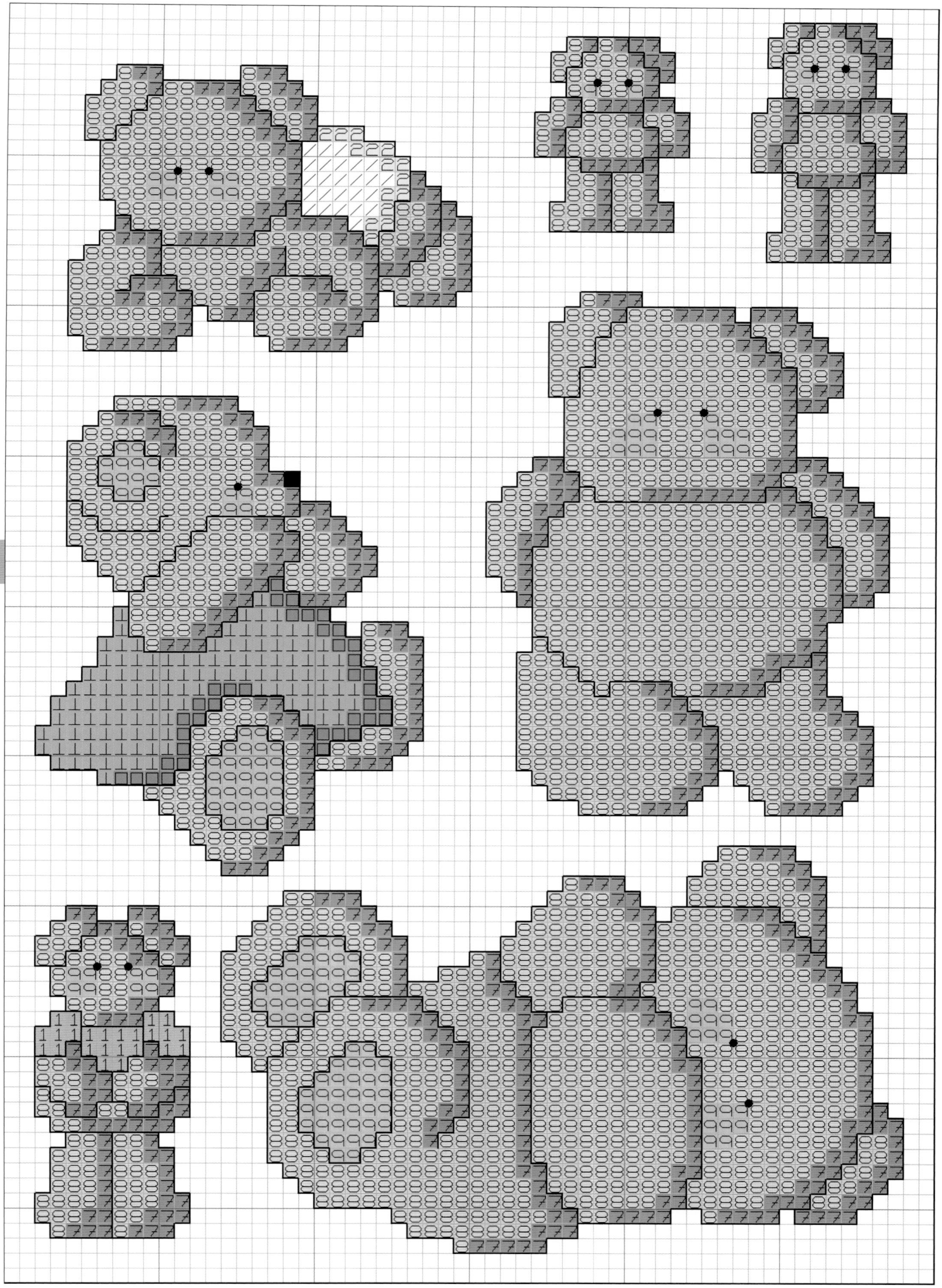

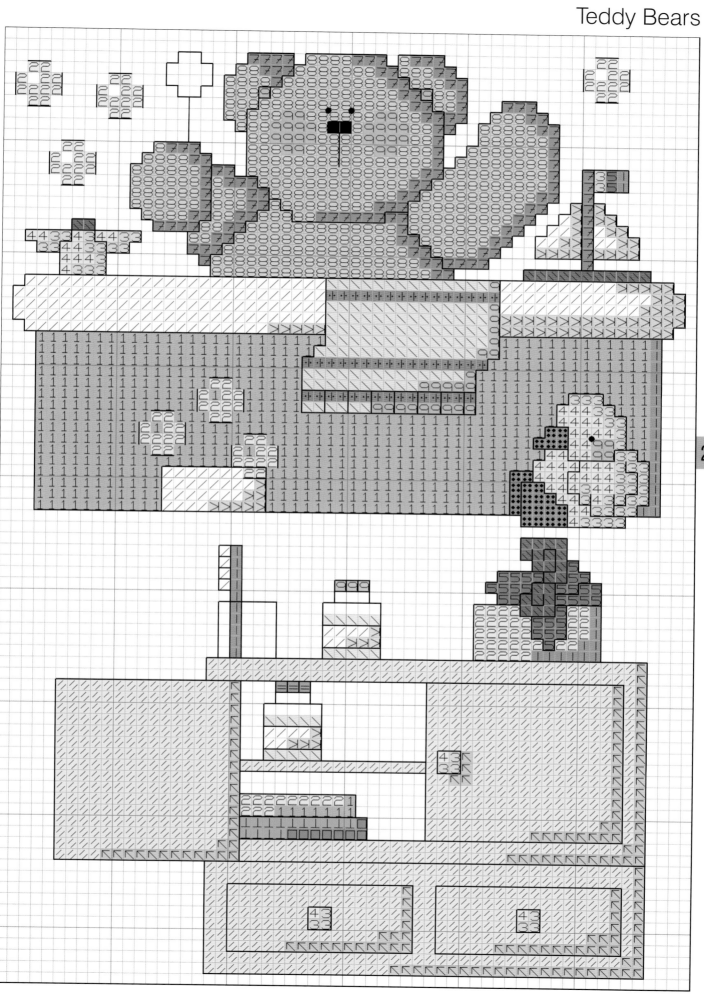

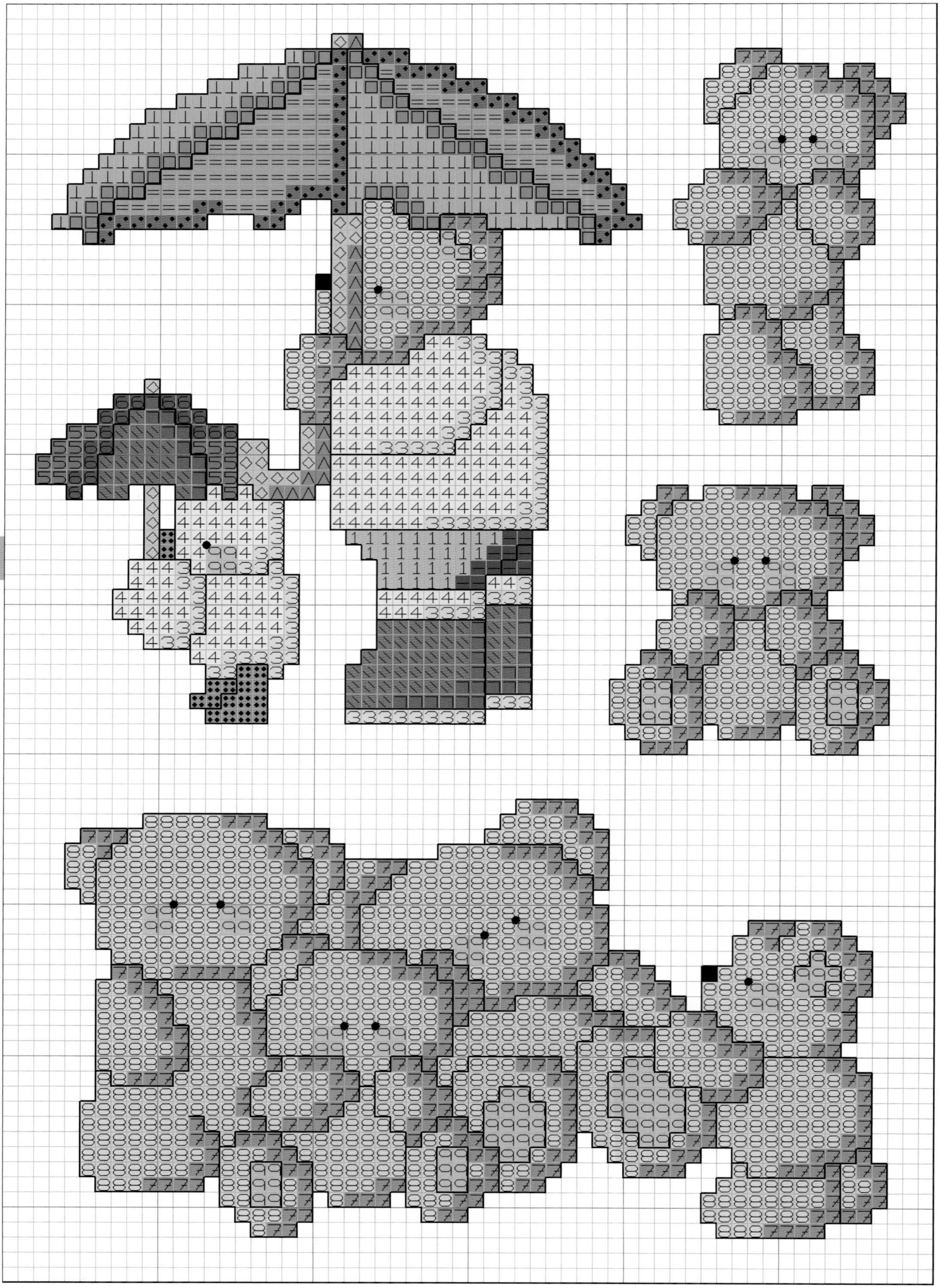

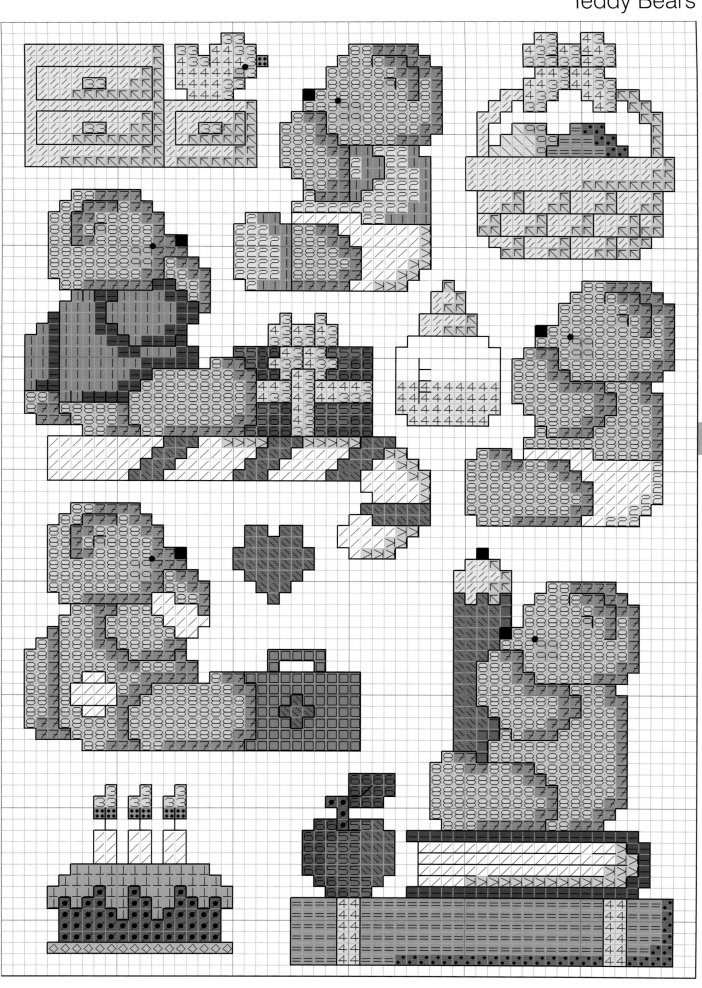

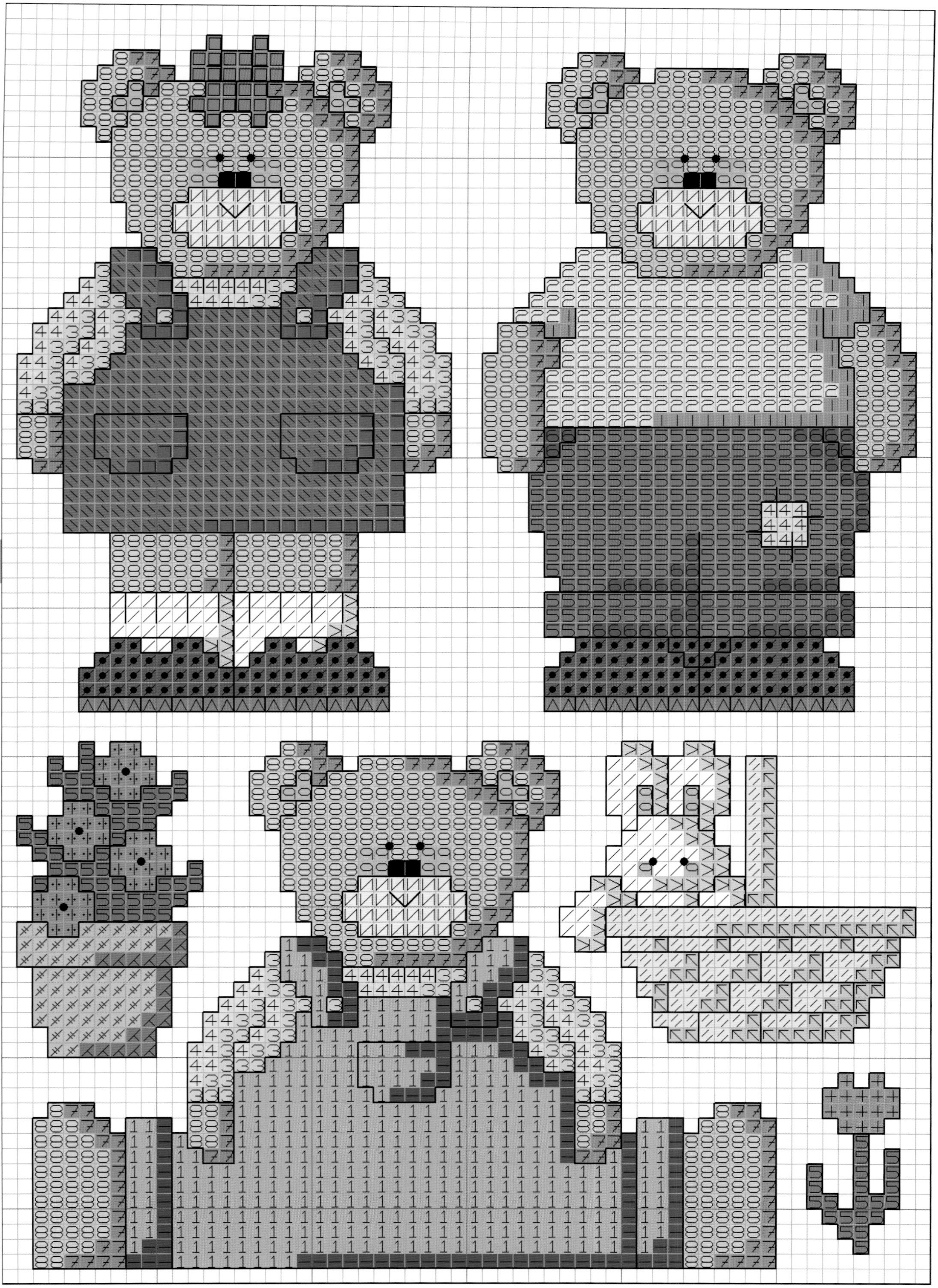

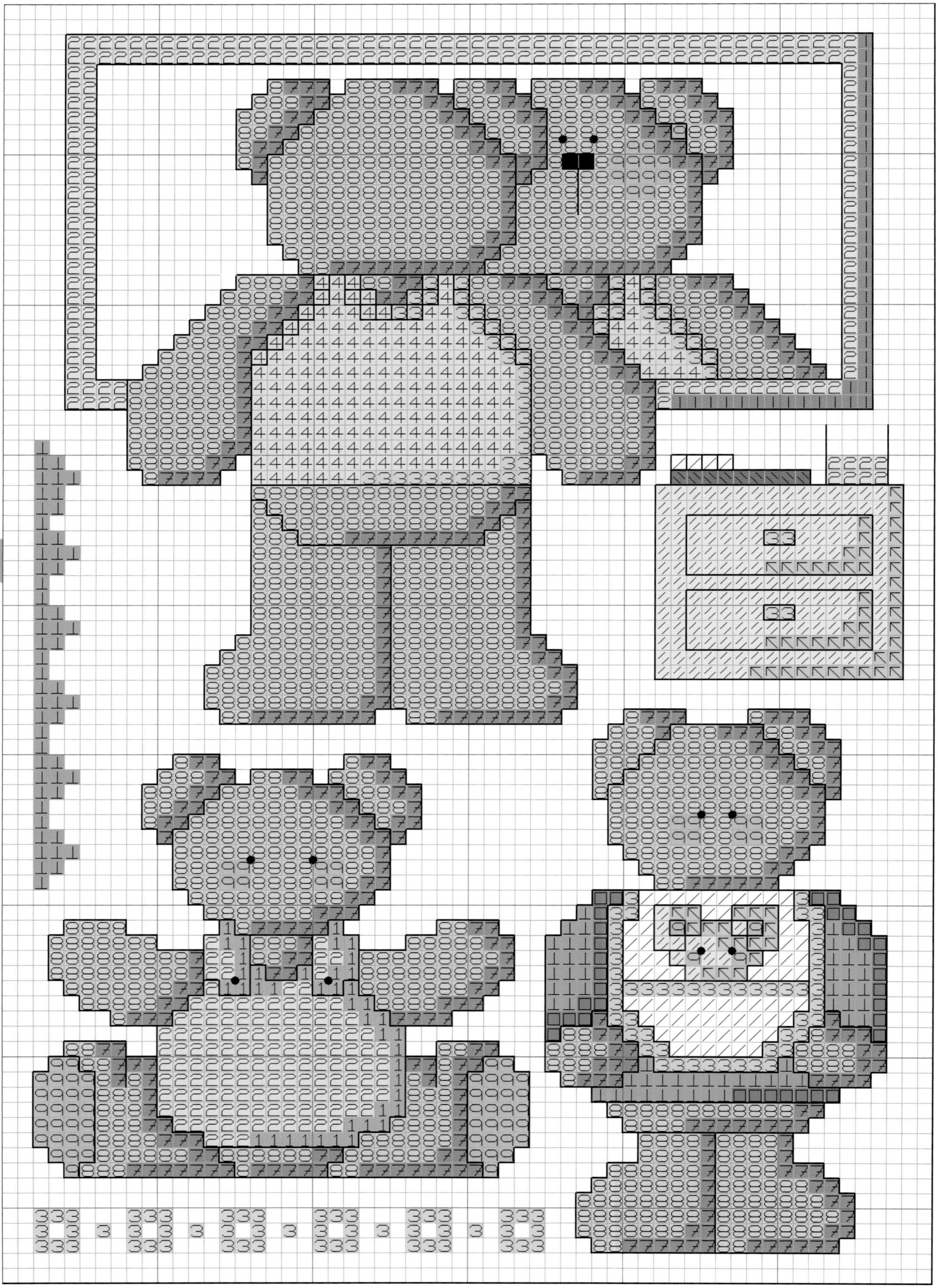

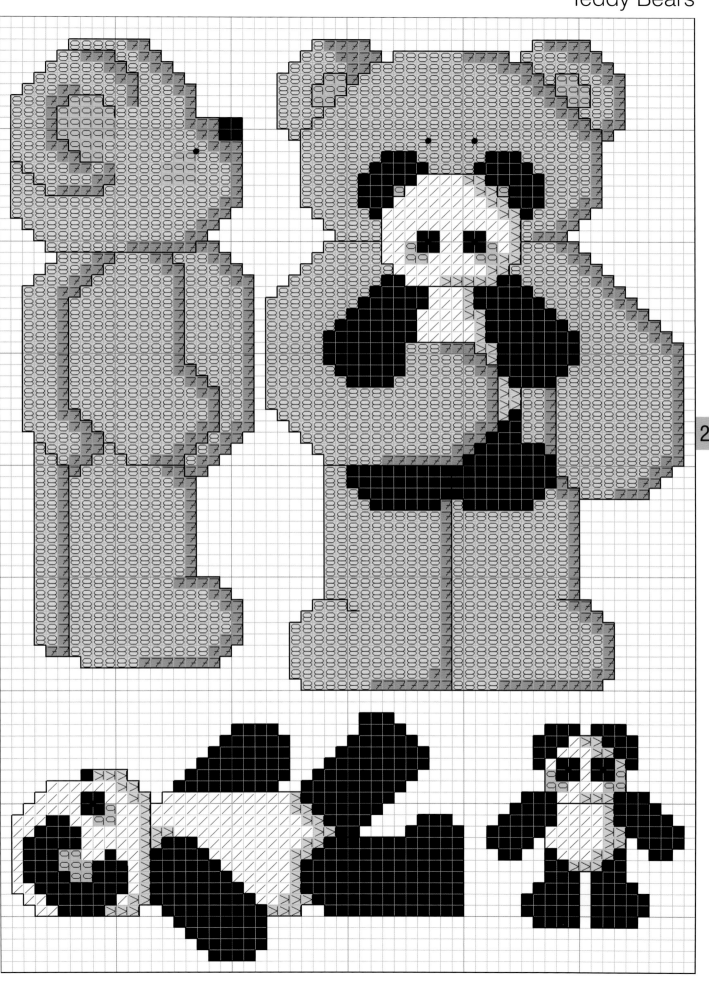

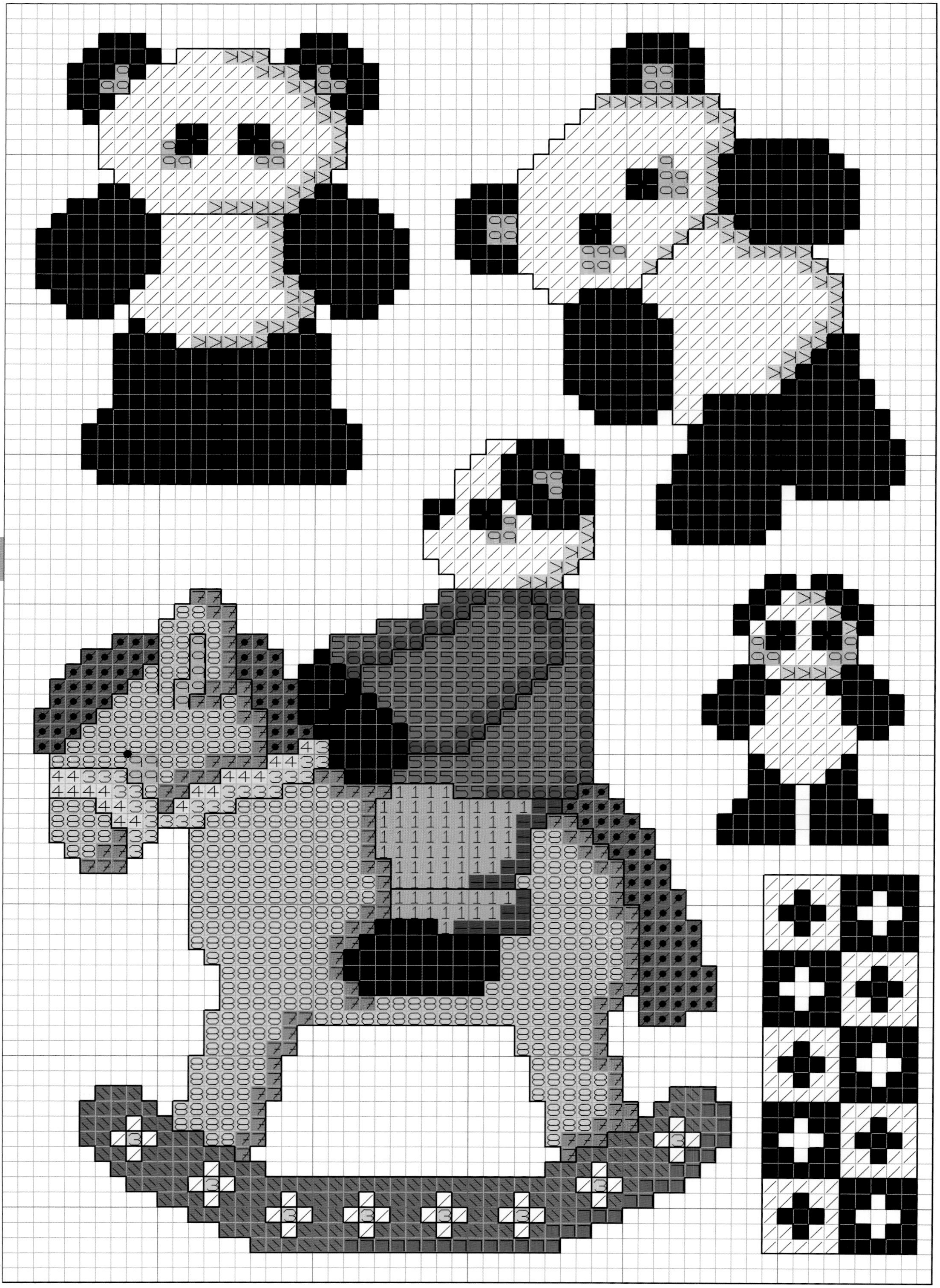

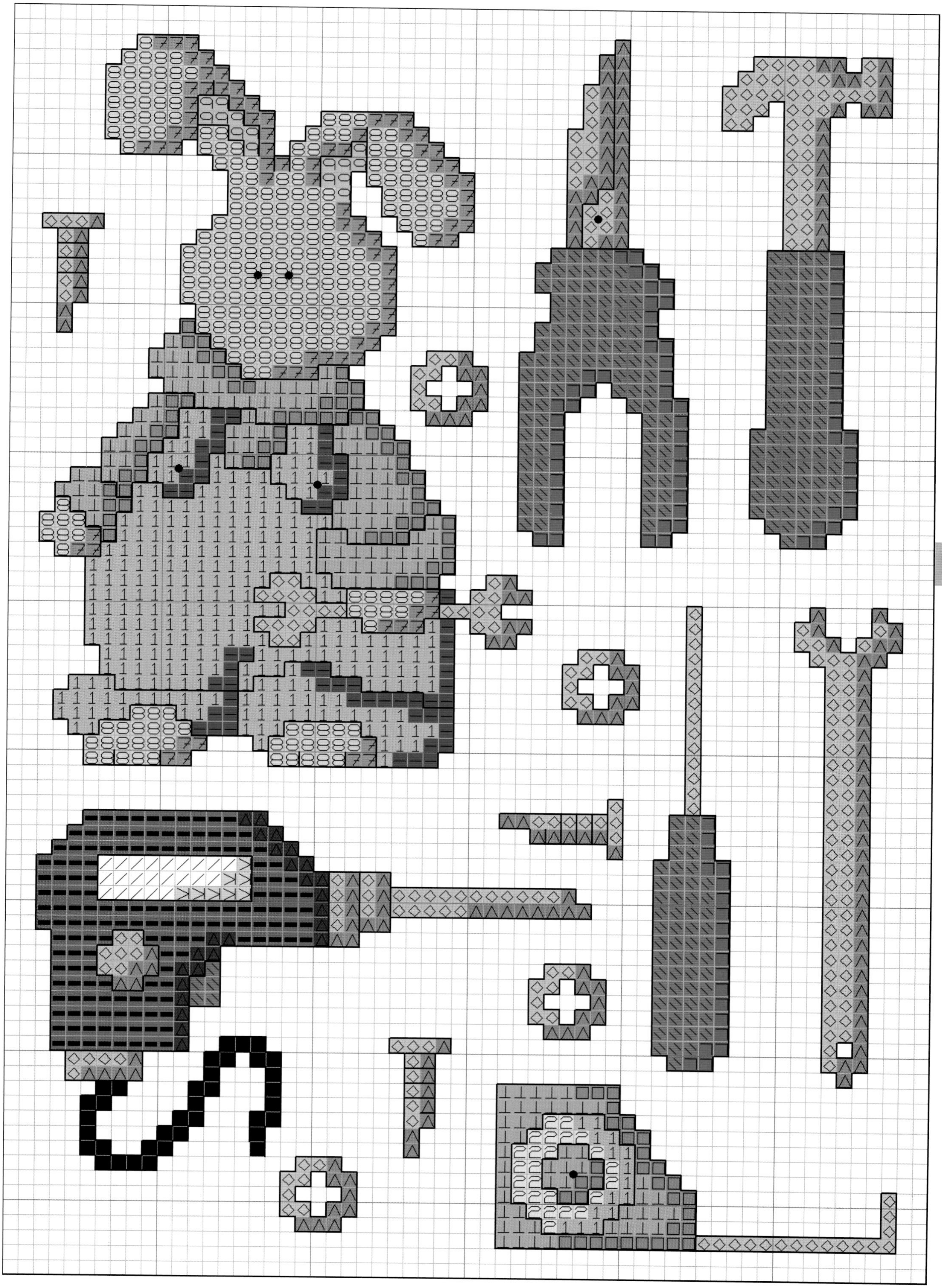

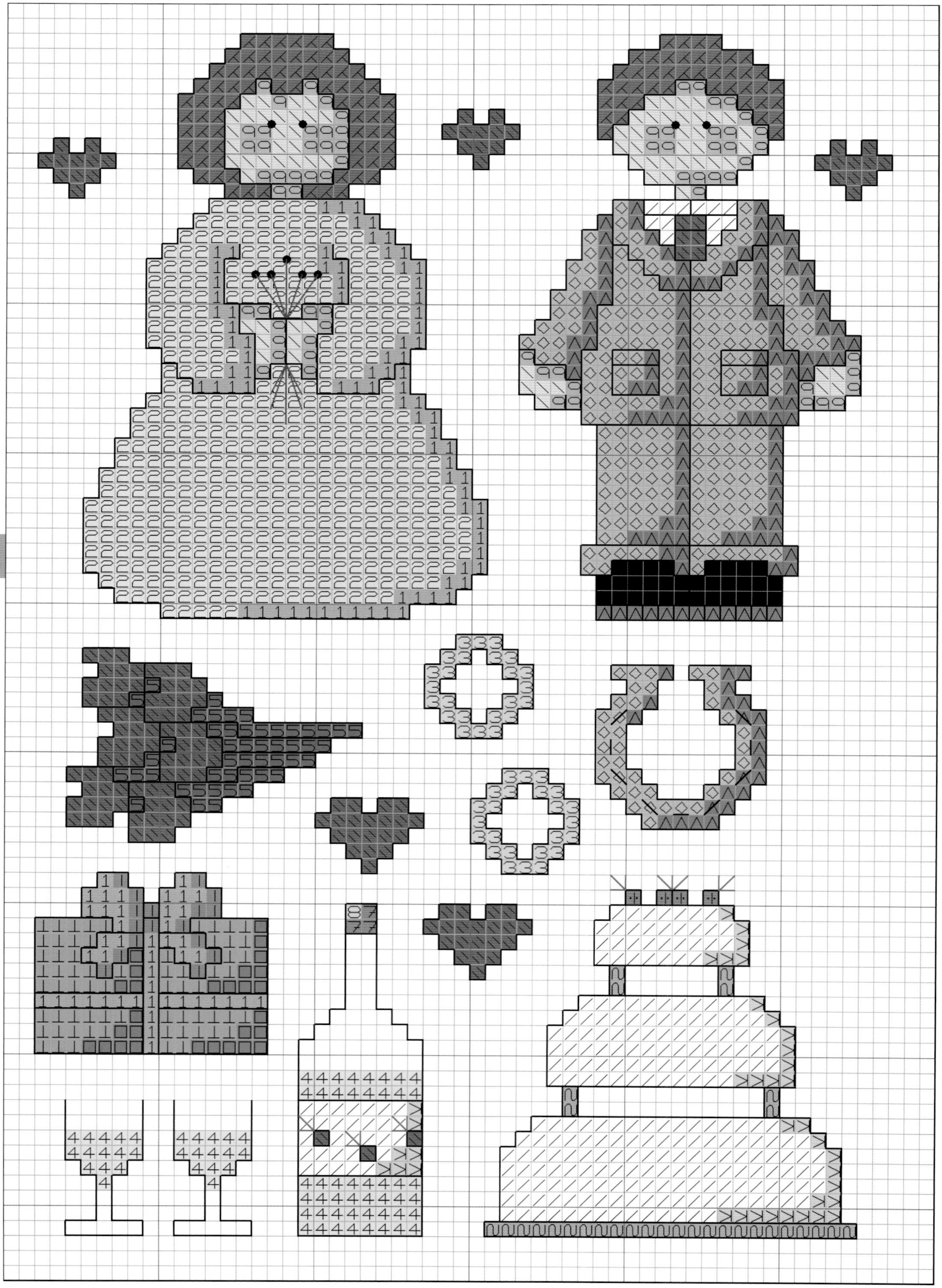

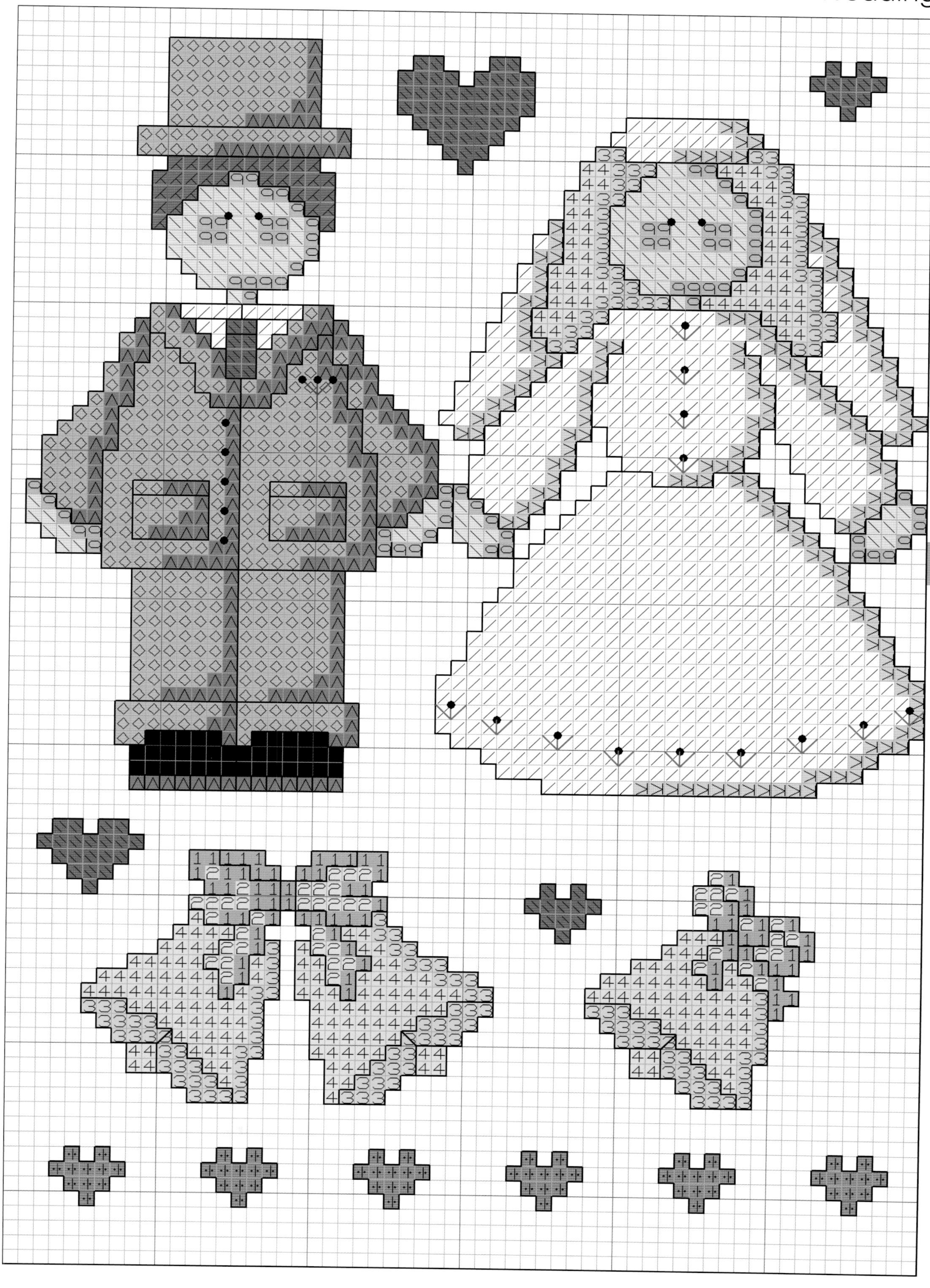

Zodiac

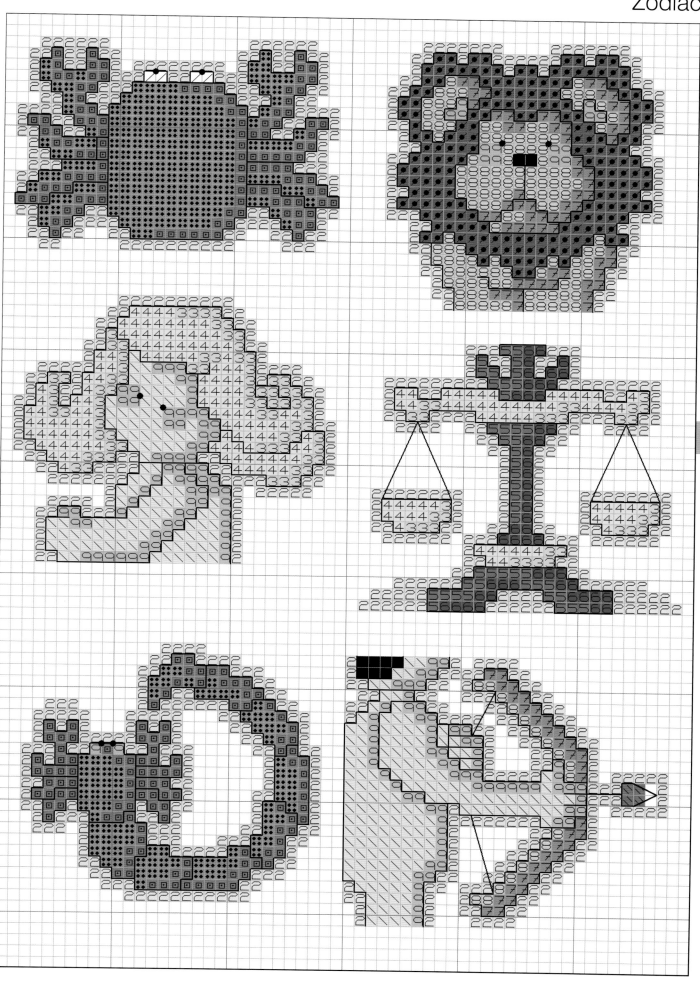

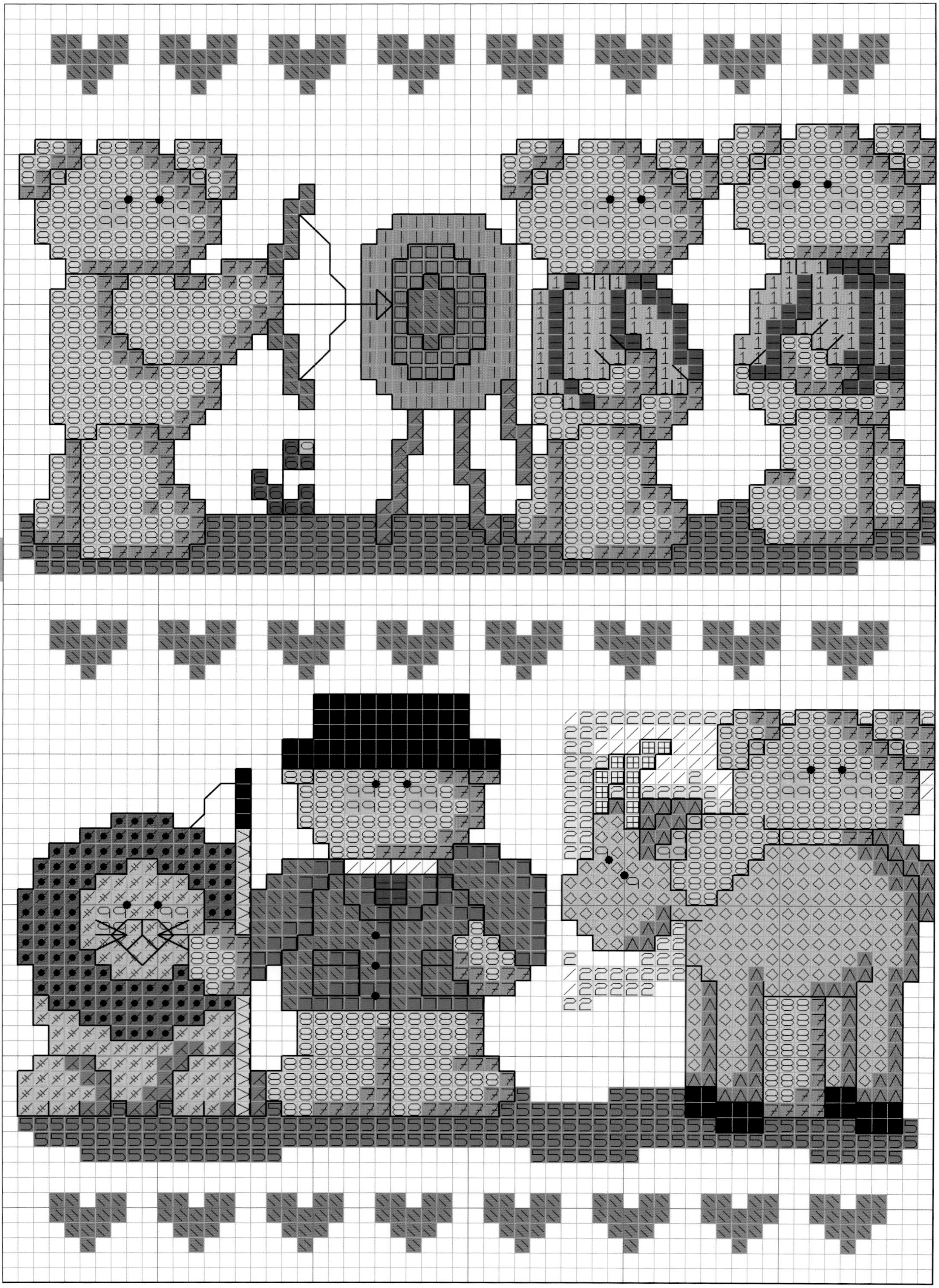

DMC Threads

The threads are all named and coded below, making the choosing of your colours easier. When you are happy with your motif designs, match your thread colours to the charts, or create your own palette. If you want to use your own colours, make a key like this to help you when you are stitching.

Symbol	Name	Code
■	Black	310
▽	Very light grey	762
⋈	Light grey	168
◇	Grey	415
∧	Dark grey	318
∩	Metallic silver	5283
/	White	B5200
\	Light pink	818
ᴘ	Pink	957
⋅ǀ⋅	Dark pink	956
\	Red	606
▬	Dark red	817
⊞	Peach	951
↓	Dark peach	3856
⫽	Very pale orange	3823
⼎	Pale orange	3855
⁚⁚	Orange	740
⊡	Dark orange	947
▬	Dark blue	798
ǀ	Blue	799
1	Light blue	809
2	Very light blue	800

Symbol	Name	Code
+	Lilac	340
○	Dark lilac	3837
⬩•	Dark purple	553
=	Purple	554
÷	Gold metallic	5282
⊖	Dark yellow	444
3	Yellow	307
4	Light yellow	727
⊥	Very light green	955
□	Light green	954
5	Green	703
6	Dark green	701
▬	Khaki green	470
▲	Dark khaki green	469
⋇	Terracotta	402
⟋	Dark terracotta	3776
⬗	Light brown	435
⟨	Brown	434
◼	Dark brown	433
7	Dark beige	436
8	Beige	738
⋈	Light beige	739

Index

255

256